School

OF THE
PROPHETS

Other Books and Materials by Kris Vallotton

Developing a Supernatural Lifestyle: A Practical Guide to a Life of Signs, Wonders, and Miracles

Fashioned to Reign: Empowering Women to Fulfill Their Divine Destiny (book, workbook, leader's guide and video segments available individually, or as an all-inclusive curriculum kit)

God's Most Beautiful Creation (a six-part DVD or CD teaching series on women)

Heavy Rain: Renew the Church, Transform the World

Moral Revolution: The Naked Truth about Sexual Purity

Outrageous Courage: What God Can Do with Raw Obedience and Radical Faith (the Tracy Evans story; co-authored with Jason Vallotton)

School of the Prophets: Advanced Training for Prophetic Ministry (book, workbook, leader's guide and video segments available, or an all-inclusive curriculum kit)

Spirit Wars: Winning the Invisible Battle against Sin and the Enemy (book, workbook, leader's guide and video segments available, or an all-inclusive curriculum kit)

The Supernatural Power of Forgiveness: Discover How to Escape Your Prison of Pain and Unlock a Life of Freedom (co-authored with Jason Vallotton)

The Supernatural Ways of Royalty: Discovering Your Rights and Privileges of Being a Son or Daughter of God (co-authored with Bill Johnson)

Basic Training for the Supernatural Ways of Royalty (workbook)

Basic Training for the Prophetic Ministry (workbook)

WORKBOOK

School
OF THE
PROPHETS

Advanced Training for Prophetic Ministry

KRIS VALLOTTON

Chosen
a division of Baker Publishing Group
Minneapolis, Minnesota

Published by Chosen Books
11400 Hampshire Avenue South
Bloomington, Minnesota 55438
www.chosenbooks.com

Chosen Books is a division of
Baker Publishing Group, Grand Rapids, Michigan

Printed in the United States of America

ISBN 978-0-8007-9623-5

Cover design by Dan Pitts

15 16 17 18 19 20 21   7 6 5 4 3 2 1

*I would like to thank Trish Konieczny
for her excellent work on this
curriculum project.*

Contents

A NEW WORLD

I wrote the book *School of the Prophets: Advanced Training for Prophetic Ministry* as a way of sharing what I have learned in 25 years of pastoring prophetic people. I will cover a lot of ground with you in the pages ahead, and we will also navigate what I refer to as some prophetic white water. If there is anything I have learned about the area of prophecy, it is that the adventure never ends. There is always more to learn. Mine is just one perspective, but I trust that you will find my insights and stories in this study helpful.

We will also talk about developing healthy prophetic communities, which is a vital necessity that is sometimes overlooked because of misunderstanding or misinformation. Prophets, prophetesses and especially those in leadership in this area must develop wholesome prophetic cultures that inspire prophetic people to be developed and deployed for the Kingdom. In fact, a solid, thriving prophetic community will help equip saints of every calling to carry the light of the Kingdom over all the earth. That is one of our major roles as prophets and prophetesses. Another major role is to bring the ministry of reconciliation to those in need as we dig for buried treasures in the dirt of broken people's lives. The lost and hurting need to see the love of the Father revealed to them through the powerful ministry of the prophetic.

Whether you hold the office of a prophet or prophetess or operate in a prophetic gift from time to time, I hope my voice of experience will encourage and exhort you in your life and ministry. I think this study will also be of value to you if the prophetic ministry is new or unfamiliar to you because you have not yet learned much about it or have not been involved with it before now. And although I focus on how the principles I present directly relate to the prophetic, many of my topics apply to other areas of ministry as well. For example, developing healthy Kingdom core values from which we live and minister is important for all of us as believers. Whatever your divine call, I pray that this study will help you play your part well in ushering in the Kingdom on earth as it is in heaven.

I will be the first to say that pastoring prophetic people can be a challenge at times; in the book I compare it to herding cats. But it is a job worth doing well. Prophets and prophetesses come with different personality profiles and come out of different prophetic streams, and they are often extraordinarily sensitive and are unaccustomed to having others speak into their lives. Many pastors are even hesitant about providing leadership to the prophetic contingent in their churches. Yet the prophetic people among us desperately need qualified leaders. Those in the office of a prophet or prophetess—which differs from operating in the gift—need input from the other fivefold ministers (apostles, evangelists, pastors and teachers) to sharpen and nourish them.

May God give each of us wisdom as we move through this study into a new world of prophetic realities. May He grant us a new understanding of both the office and the gift, and may He help us understand our times and how we should act in them so that we have the most effect for His Kingdom. May we go forth in the power of His Spirit as He strategically places us all over the earth to dispel the darkness and bring hope to the hurting and healing to the nations.

TRAINING FOR THE PROPHETIC

How to Use This Curriculum

This workbook is divided into eight sessions that will take you deeper into the topics I explore in my book *School of the Prophets: Advanced Training for Prophetic Ministry*. Each session will take five days to go through, and each day lists different readings for you from Scripture and from the book. Each day also provides questions for you to answer that will help you think through what you are learning as you discover more about the role of prophets and prophetesses in our day and the ways in which we can develop healthy prophetic communities within our churches.

Move through the daily readings at a thoughtful pace, praying that the Holy Spirit will become your teacher and "guide you into all truth" (John 16:13). Approach the questions with an open heart and an open ear, listening for the Holy Spirit's input and direction as you process the information and insights I provide about the prophetic ministry and its place in both the past and in the present day.

At the end of each session, there is also a life application that helps you take what you learned in that session and apply it to your life in a specific, concrete way. I believe that knowledge is valuable and that increasing our knowledge about spiritual things is important. I am a strong supporter of serious scholarship, and I helped found and currently oversee the Bethel School of Supernatural Ministry. But while educating ourselves about spiritual things is crucial, it can only take us so far, unless we take what we know and make application with it. To *know* something and to *do* something about it are two entirely different things. Application is an important part of any study—probably the most important part. I urge you to take concrete steps to apply what you are learning in this study by following through with each session's life application. (If you are part of a *School of the Prophets* study group, make sure to implement the life applications before your group meetings so that you can discuss the results.)

Note that I did not put together the readings, questions and life applications in this workbook as a means of adding to your daily busywork. We all have enough busywork! I designed this workbook so that you can skip one day and come back the next if needed, or do two days at a time and still get through each session in about a week. Each day's readings and questions should take only twenty or thirty minutes of your time, and I think you will find that the results will be well worth it.

Keep in mind that as with any curriculum, you will get out of this study what you put into it. Stay faithful in doing the daily lessons, and stick with me from beginning to end. If you will do that, I believe the results will encourage and empower you, whether you hold the office of a prophet or prophetess, whether you move in a prophetic gift or whether you just want to learn more about this exciting area of ministry in the Church and in the world today. This study will give you a good understanding of the prophetic ministry and provide you with some advanced training in this area.

While you can use the *School of the Prophets* book and workbook at home to study these things on your own, you will also see that there is a video guide at the end of each workbook section. Those fill-in-the-blank guides are included because I have recorded a series of eight video segments that go along with these materials. In the video segments, which are geared for use in a small group setting, I have added a lot more depth and clarification to each section. You can purchase and view the videos yourself, which will greatly enhance what you gain from this study. They were designed, however, to promote fellowship with other believers as you walk through this study together and pray for and encourage each other. It is ideal to become part of a group that will use the *School of the Prophets* book, workbook and video segments as tools to inform and educate everyone in the group and to foster discussion about how each of you can apply what you are learning most effectively. I urge you to join a *School of the Prophets* study group if one is available at your church or somewhere nearby. If you cannot find such a group, you can host one. A *School of the Prophets Curriculum Kit* for group leaders is also available to help you do just that.

DISCOVERING YOUR DIVINE CALL

I started proactively pastoring our prophetic people about 25 years ago . . . through the years I have learned to enjoy every prophetic stream and the variety of ways that God speaks to people in various epoch seasons, and through diverse cultural experiences and core values. I have come to understand that each of us views the Kingdom through a glass dimly, yet our collective perspectives are much more accurate because revelation is actually a community garden. It is cultivated, seeded, weeded and harvested by a prophetic community and not by an isolated island dweller. It is therefore imperative that prophets and prophetesses develop wholesome prophetic communities that inspire healthy young prophets and prophetic people to be discovered, developed and ultimately deployed into their divine destinies.

The challenge with leading a diverse group of prophetic people is that it is often like herding cats!

School of the Prophets, page 19

—— DAY 1 ——

COLLECTIVE PERSPECTIVES

For now we see in a mirror dimly, but then face to face; now I know in part, but then I will know fully.

1 Corinthians 13:12

The river of revelation that flows from heaven to earth is mighty, and navigating its surging white waters is both adventurous and challenging. More than one prophetic stream feeds into this mighty river, each with a strong current of its own. The power of these streams increases exponentially when they join together, and the result is sometimes a wild ride.

Of course, my experience with God was a wild ride right from the start. Hearing His audible voice in response to my desperate prayer as a teen, seeing my mother instantly healed and finding myself in the Jesus People movement early on was all more than I bargained for, but He always gives us more than we can ask or imagine (see Ephesians 3:20). I tell you more about my salvation story in today's reading from *School of the Prophets*.

I also tell you more about the different streams of the prophetic that I have experienced since then, and I talk about the value and diversity of each. Bill Johnson, senior leader of my church, Bethel Church in Redding, California, has helped me with his balanced perspective on the prophetic ministry and his understanding of its various streams. "Eat the meat and spit out the bones" was his constant refrain to me as I began to work more and more in the area of pastoring our prophetic people.

When you work to develop a healthy prophetic community, as I am doing at Bethel, it really can feel as if you are herding cats—but it is a job worth doing. Whatever our prophetic background, each of us sees in a mirror dimly. Joined together in community, however, our collective perspectives bring God's revelation into sharper focus for all of us.

As you read *School of the Prophets* and work through this curriculum, my hope is that it will sharpen your focus on the prophetic and give you new tools and insights to use as you take your own ride down the white waters of God's river of revelation.

- Today's Scripture reading: Ephesians 4:11–16
- Today's reading from *School of the Prophets*: pages 15–20

Questions to Consider _____

1. Which three of the prophetic streams—the Jesus People movement, the charismatic Catholics or the Pentecostals—have you had the most experience with? What strengths do you think that one lends to our overall prophetic culture?

2. What do you think Bill Johnson's advice to "eat the meat and spit out the bones" means in relation to prophetic diversity? In what ways might it also relate to other areas of the Church?

3. How does having a collective perspective within a prophetic community strengthen it?

4. I mention in today's book reading that pastors tend to be afraid of prophetically gifted people. Nonetheless, why do prophets and prophetesses need pastoral leadership and input from the other fivefold ministers? (See *School of the Prophets* page 20.)

— DAY 2 —
TIME WILL TELL. . . .

Eye has not seen, nor ear heard, nor have entered into the heart of man the things which God has prepared for those who love Him.

1 Corinthians 2:9 NKJV

I thought hearing God speak audibly to me when I was a teenager was a shock—until the day in 1985 when Jesus walked into my bathroom while I was reading the Bible in the bathtub. And the things He told me on that visit were inconceivable—until the day when I started to see them come to pass in my life.

For a long time I kept quiet about the things the Lord told me, concerned on the one hand that some people would think I was crazy, and on the other hand that my practical wife would start looking for ways to get on with them. (Kathy is not one to sit around when there is something to be done.) After a while, I figured time would tell if the visitation was real or if I had imagined it. But I could not get away from what the Lord had said about that very thing before He walked out of the bathroom: *History will tell us if you believe Me!*

I had to start somewhere, even though I had no idea how to become what the Lord had told me I would be. How does a simple auto mechanic become a prophet to the nations and go before kings and queens? I decided the best thing I could do was study Scripture and everything else I could get my hands on about prophets and prophecy. (Maybe that same kind of decision on your part is why you are reading these pages right now.) I soaked up the information like a sponge, and it lit in me a passion for the prophetic. The rest, as they say, is history.

- Today's Scripture reading: 1 Corinthians 2:6–16
- Today's reading from *School of the Prophets*: pages 21–26

Questions to Consider _____

1. Has the Lord ever told you something (not necessarily audibly or in a visitation) that seemed inconceivable to you? Was your reaction anything like mine? In what ways have you begun to see that word come to pass? If you are still waiting to see its fulfillment, what are you doing in the meantime to prepare for it?

   _____

   _____

   _____

2. Sometimes practical people like Kathy spend less time questioning words from the Lord and more time getting them done. Do you lean toward the practical or the analytical personality? How does this affect your response to the prophetic?

   _____

   _____

   _____

3. What do you do when your emotions are all over the map about something God has shown you, as mine were after God called me as a prophet to the nations? Where do you find stability in the middle of excitement and terror and concern and questioning?

   _____

   _____

   _____

4. Days turned into months and years as the vision I had seen grew in my heart and began to produce fruit. It was a process. We will spend more than one lesson in the days ahead talking about how it is a process to the palace, so to speak. Briefly describe a time when you had to have some patience as you walked through a spiritual process.

   _____

   _____

   _____

—— Day 3 ——

Established by Grace

A man's gift makes room for him and brings him before great men.

Proverbs 18:16

It takes some time for your gift to make room for you and bring you before great leaders. If you are patient in the process, by His grace God will establish you in your divine call. More than two decades passed between the time I was called as a prophet and the time I began to move into the authority that position would bring me.

That kind of time frame is not unusual. Look at the story of David's kingship, which I talk about in today's book reading. Three different times he was anointed as king, but the interval between the anointing and the crown was a long one for him. Jesus Himself took some time to grow into His calling, increasing in wisdom and stature and favor with God and man. If it was a process for Him, you know it will be a process for us!

I had more than a few anxious moments in the process I went through before I realized that it was a matter of letting God promote me among my peers and waiting for the favor of those in leadership around me. Once God established me in their eyes, they acknowledged my prophetic calling and recognized my position in the church. From there, I was able to move into a new level of ministry and authority.

If you are called as a prophet or prophetess, keep in mind that until you go through the process of letting God establish you in your calling, you are only a prophet to yourself. And you know what leadership expert John Maxwell says. I quote him in *School of the Prophets*, but I will quote him here, too: "He who thinks he leads, but has no followers, is only taking a walk." Trying to rush the process of being established as a prophet or prophetess does not work—but that is a topic for tomorrow's lesson.

- Today's Scripture reading: 1 Samuel 16; Romans 13:1–7
- Today's reading from *School of the Prophets*: pages 26–32

Questions to Consider _____

1. Jesus said that "a prophet is not without honor except in his hometown and in his own household" (Matthew 13:57). In what ways have you seen that come to pass? Have you ever seen it misapplied, for example as the basis of an insecure prophet's persecution complex?

   _____

   _____

   _____

2. Have you ever been put in the position of wondering if a prophetic word you gave would prove wrong, as I was with the prophecy I gave to Bethel's staff about the prayer chapel offering? What kind of things ran through your mind in that moment? How did God vindicate your prophetic declaration?

   _____

   _____

   _____

3. Why isn't some sort of prophetic word or personal experience of "being commissioned as a prophet" a license to operate in the office of prophet in a local church or ministry? What more does it take to be established and effective?

   _____

   _____

   _____

4. How did David show great patience in the process on his way to be-coming king? How did he show respect even for leadership who did not acknowledge his divine call? (See *School of the Prophets* pages 31–32.)

   _____

   _____

   _____

— Day 4 —
Stay Out of the Pit

God is opposed to the proud, but gives grace to the humble.

James 4:6

Self-promotion always lands us in a pit. It is a dangerous thing. These days, it is also a common thing. Just think of all the so-called experts out there who are engaged in self-promotion through social networking and other online avenues. The possibilities are endless, particularly for charlatans and deceivers.

But the world is not the only place where self-promotion runs rampant. It can also be found in the Church. Countless believers have gotten themselves into trouble—gotten themselves thrown in a pit, so to speak—because they tried to promote themselves into positions of authority and influence before the time was right.

I am amazed by the number of prophetic people who land themselves in a pit that way. They may claim that other people threw them in as a result of misguided persecution, but if you ask me, they helped them to it. It is kind of like the Old Testament story of Joseph, which I talk about in today's book reading. Scripture tells us that Joseph's brothers threw him in a pit before selling him into slavery. While that is true, I think Joseph helped them to it. By trying to take authority over them before they were ready for him to lead, he gave his brothers some serious reasons to get frustrated with him.

Sometimes we in the Church do the same thing. We attempt to establish ourselves in a prophetic position before the time is right, and the net result is never good. We just talked in Day 3 about how we are established by grace.

We need to wait for favor—both the favor of God and the favor of others—and let divine promotion, not self-promotion, take us where we need to be. Let God promote and establish you. That is the way to stay out of the pit.

- Today's Scripture reading: Genesis 37; 2 Samuel 15:1–14
- Today's reading from *School of the Prophets*: pages 33–35

Questions to Consider _____

1. In today's reading from *School of the Prophets*, I state that there were many paths Joseph could have taken to the palace, without necessarily landing in a pit. Describe a time when you looked up from the bottom of a pit, spiritually speaking, and thought, *There must have been an easier path I could have taken to get where I'm going!*

2. How do you think the verse I quoted at the beginning of today's lesson, James 4:6, applies to the office of the prophet? (See *School of the Prophets* page 34.)

3. In attempting to promote himself, David's son Absalom displayed a political spirit that was divisive and devastating. Have you seen evidence of that spirit still wreaking havoc today (either in the Church or outside it), as I have? What do you think lies at the root of that spirit?

4. What are the possible results of self-promotion when a person has favor with God, but not man? What are the possible results of self-promotion when a person has favor with man, but not God?

DAY 5

PREMATURE PROMOTION PROBLEMS

Do not lay hands upon anyone too hastily.

1 Timothy 5:22

I believe that when God promotes us, He protects us. The protection comes with the position. That is not to say we won't face new battles in new positions, but our protection and the weapons of our warfare will be as mighty as we need them to be.

The problem comes in, of course, when we promote ourselves. There is such a thing as promoting ourselves beyond our God-given protection. Another word for that is presumption—not to mention foolishness.

What happens, though, if our leadership promotes us prematurely by asking us to step into a position we are not yet ready for? What I call "eager beaver" leaders in the Church do that all the time in an attempt to stay current or ride some new spiritual wave. The results are no less devastating. In fact, they are multiplied because they now affect both the prophetic person who is being promoted and the congregation under his or her undeveloped, immature influence.

There is no substitute for the process of preparation it takes to fulfill a governmental office in the Church. A person needs to develop the character and skills necessary, and that can take time and experience. You cannot bypass the process and expect the end results to be the same. That is why I think Paul urged Timothy over and over again to use wisdom and take care in promoting people within the Church. Wise leaders must see that the people whom they promote into leadership, whether in the prophetic realm or in another area of Church governance, are well equipped to wear the mantles for which God has destined them.

- Today's Scripture reading: 1 Timothy 3:1–13
- Today's reading from *School of the Prophets*: pages 36–38

Questions to Consider

1. In what ways does the popular expression "greater levels, greater devils" fail to take into account the way our level of protection goes up with our level of God-given promotion? (See *School of the Prophets* page 36.)

2. What happens to the adequacy of our protection if we presumptuously promote ourselves? How can this result in living in a constant state of turmoil?

3. Have you met any "eager beaver" Church leaders or even leaders in the business world who caused themselves and those around them difficulties by promoting someone prematurely? Have you been an "eager beaver" in this area? What painful lessons were learned from the events that transpired?

4. How do you think premature installation into the office of a prophet or prophetess might be unhealthy for someone? What about for those around him or her? What are some of the ways Church leadership can safeguard against such a situation?

■ Session 1 Life Application _____

We talked a lot in this first session about how a process of preparation usually is necessary before someone is ready to fulfill a governmental office in the Church. In the sessions ahead, we will look at some of the specifics involved in preparing for prophetic ministry, but just now, think about an area in which you already hold a position of some authority. (It can be in the Church, in the workplace or in your personal or family life.) What were some of the things that prepared you to lead well in that area? In what ways were you ill-prepared? Ask the Holy Spirit to show you how you can continue to grow in your ability to minister to others through your leadership.

Here is a harder question that will require some soul-searching on your part: Did self-promotion play any part in gaining your position of authority? Did you advance ahead of either the favor of God or the favor of others (their readiness to let you lead)? What kind of problems did that cause? Did you wind up at the bottom of a pit after stepping out from under God's protection? Since God is taking us from glory to glory and undoubtedly has more for you to accomplish, how can you avoid the painful problems of self-promotion the next time around?

■ **Session 1 Video Guide** _____

1. You shouldn't be _____ when you're praying and _____ shows up.

2. It's not good to _____ with the Lord; you can learn that from reading the _____.

3. If you will spend your _____ bringing out the _____ in people, you will always have a _____.

4. "He who _____ a prophet in the name of a prophet shall receive a prophet's _____" (Matthew 10:41).

5. If God calls you, when it's time for Him to _____ you for that position, He will create some kind of _____, some kind of _____, some kind of place—something that says to the rest of the people, "This person is called for this time to this people for this ministry."

6. When you are anointed, God will create a _____ from the _____ to the _____.

NEW VERSUS OLD TESTAMENT PROPHETS

We are the revelation (light) of the Father and His love letter to the world. We "re-present" Christ to the lost. The lost look to us when they are trying to understand world events through the eyes of God. When we misrepresent our heavenly Father, the world gets a warped perspective of God. . . .

One of the greatest tragedies in the world comes from negative prophetic voices who misrepresent God. Their declarations cause the lost to believe that our Father is an angry God looking for an opportunity to punish people. Jesus said, "If the light that is in you is darkness, how great is the darkness!" (Matthew 6:23). If we who are the light of the world are speaking and prophesying against people who are lost in darkness, how great is the darkness!

School of the Prophets, pages 48–49

— Day 1 —

Calling Down Fire

Many false prophets will arise and deceive many; and because of
the increase of evildoing, the love of many will grow cold.

Matthew 24:11–12

Many prophetic people I have met long for the days when the
prophets of old called down fire from heaven to deal with evil.
Curses and judgments and famines and droughts showed sinners
what was what, and if that did not work, there was always genocide. Many
of the same prophetic people are asking today, why shouldn't those kinds
of spiritual cleansings take place in our time and simplify our efforts to deal
with the evils of society? I call those people the "Prophets of Doom." They
make it hard for unbelievers to view the Church of today as the "House of
Hope," which is what it should be seen as.

I sympathize that many of our prophetic role models in Scripture are
of the Old Testament/judgment/punishment era, so I can see why some of
the prophets of today are tempted to build their "ministries" around that
model. But they forget to take into account that today is a new day. Christ
established a New Covenant that calls for mercy toward those in need of Him.

It is hard to extend mercy, though, when you are busy calling down fire
to consume evildoers where they stand. I think of the travesty of 9-11, the
day the Twin Towers fell in New York City. What good came of telling so
many people already beset by loss and grief that their loved ones died in a
judgment sent down from above by an angry God? Did that pronouncement
really advance the Kingdom of heaven on earth? Not that I can see.

I think there is a difference between a thirst for righteousness and a thirst for judgment. And sometimes I think a lot of prophetic people do not know the difference. We need to focus less on calling down fire and more on calling down mercy. In the days ahead in this session, we are going to take a closer look at why.

- Today's Scripture reading: 1 Kings 18
- Today's reading from *School of the Prophets*: pages 39–44

Questions to Consider _____

1. Why do you think that even for the merciful among us, the mere thought of judging the wicked can be inspiring? What is it in us that makes us thirst to see others fall under judgment?

_____

_____

_____

2. I start today's book reading by saying that in the twenty-first century, there is much confusion over the office of the prophet and prophetess. We will look at many of the reasons for that throughout this study, but in your eyes, what are some of the major sources of this confusion?

_____

_____

_____

3. How do the "Prophets of Doom" offset the ministry of the "House of Hope" (the Church) to unbelievers?

_____

_____

_____

4. In regard to the prophetic, what does it mean to say that even a broken watch is right twice a day? (See *School of the Prophets* page 44.)

_____

_____

_____

— DAY 2 —

SALT AND LIGHT?

I searched for a man among them who would build up the wall
and stand in the gap before Me for the land, so that I would not
destroy it; but I found no one.

Ezekiel 22:30

As daunting as the prophets of old could be, they were also called to
preserve, protect and stand in the gap for the people. Even as they
delivered the powerful Word of the Lord, they interceded with God
to seek mercy for those who did not deserve it. You might say they were the
salt of preservation and the light that revealed God's heart for the world.

Does that sound familiar, salt and light? Didn't Jesus mention something
about that in regard to our role as believers in the New Covenant? In the
same way as salt preserves food, we are the element in society that preserves
it from wrath and destruction. In the same way as light chases away darkness, we chase away the warped perspectives of God that people in darkness
have. The lost look to us when they are trying to understand world events
through His eyes, and we "re-present" Christ to the world in those moments,
spotlighting the love in His heart for them.

If we will not be the salt and light of God's Kingdom on the earth, is it
any wonder that people in darkness get the wrong idea and think God is an
angry God bent on humankind's destruction?

In reality He is patient to the core, not willing that anyone should perish,
but that all should come to repentance and a true knowledge of Him (see

2 Peter 3:9). As prophets and prophetesses, we need to ask ourselves if that is also the desire of our hearts. The answer will show just how salty and bright we are.

- Today's Scripture reading: Matthew 5:13–16; Ezekiel 18
- Today's reading from *School of the Prophets*: pages 44–49

Questions to Consider _____

1. In what ways have we become tasteless when we prophesy against the very people we are supposed to preserve? (See *School of the Prophets* pages 45–46.)

_____

_____

_____

2. How is the example of Moses we looked at in today's reading a foretaste of the influence one prophet can have on God? Why do you think God changed His mind when Moses petitioned Him?

_____

_____

_____

3. What kind of warped perspectives of God have you encountered in unbelievers? Was a misrepresentation of Him on the part of believers one root of the problem?

_____

_____

_____

4. Name some ways in which negative prophetic voices can have a negative impact on the lost rather than a positive impact.

_____

_____

_____

—— DAY 3 ——

AT THE CROSSROADS

This cup which is poured out for you is the new covenant in My blood.

Luke 22:20

The cross of Christ stood at the crossroads of all spiritual history. It was there that humankind's relationship with God took a completely different turn. At the cross, the Old Covenant gave way to the New, but before that happened, the Old Covenant served its purpose. It showed us, for one thing, how terribly ineffective our own efforts at self-righteousness would be. It showed us how very much we needed to go in a different direction. In effect, through its harshness toward sinners, the Old Covenant prepared us for the New Covenant.

It took us a long time, though, to realize how much we needed the New Covenant, which the shedding of Christ's blood on the cross made possible. In fact, many of us still do not get it. Many people beset by a religious spirit are still determined to achieve righteousness their own way.

We certainly take after Adam in that regard. All the way back to the Garden of Eden, humankind has been determined to do things its own way. Adam chose to acquire the knowledge of good and evil from the forbidden fruit, when he would have been much better off (wouldn't we all?) learning righteousness through an ongoing relationship with God.

It is, in the end, all about relationship. The Old and New Covenants are about two completely different relationships between us and God—mutually exclusive relationships. If we do not understand the difference, we can become spiritually schizophrenic prophets and prophetesses who do not understand who we are in relation to God or how we relate to Him once we pass the crossroads at the cross.

- Today's Scripture reading: Matthew 5:21–48
- Today's reading from *School of the Prophets*: pages 49–54

Questions to Consider _____

1. Why is it accurate to call the cross of Christ the crossroads of all spiritual history? What choice of direction does each person who stands at the crossroads have?

   _____

   _____

   _____

2. Why was Jesus' blood as the sacrificial Lamb necessary to inaugurate the New Covenant? What effect did His sacrifice have on the way God related to the world? (See *School of the Prophets* page 50.)

   _____

   _____

   _____

3. Why is saying that the Old Covenant is obsolete and disappearing like doing away with the Constitution of the United States and inaugurating an entirely new system of government?

   _____

   _____

   _____

4. What is mutually exclusive about the two different relationships between God and humanity pre-crossroads and post-crossroads?

   _____

   _____

   _____

5. What was it about biblical covenant that made it necessary for God to be so tough on sinners under the Old Covenant? How did God fulfill the requirements of the Law and consequently extend mercy to millions who do not deserve it under the New Covenant?

_____

_____

_____

— Day 4 —

The Book of Fugitives

He made Him who knew no sin to be sin on our behalf, so that
we might become the righteousness of God in Him.

2 Corinthians 5:21

You and I had our names written down in the Book of Fugitives from the Law, and the punishment due us was death. How could God extend mercy to us and satisfy His sense of justice as the righteous Judge? To do both seemed impossible, yet nothing is impossible with God.

In today's reading from *School of the Prophets*, I tell you an imaginative story that illustrates how God solved this seeming dilemma once and for all. It is a story of guilt, judgment and sacrifice that parallels the story of the whole human race in relationship to God.

We all start with an incredible debt of sin mounted against us, and no matter how far we try to run, we cannot remain fugitives forever. Judgment Day is coming—a day when each of us will face the just Judge of the universe. How can we avoid the death penalty that is our due?

God has a profound solution for our predicament. Because of Jesus' death on the cross, God now has the right to release each of us from the punishment we deserve without being an unjust Judge. Jesus fulfilled the cause of justice through the sacrifice of His blood on the cross, which leaves us free to go and sin no more, having become the righteousness of God in Christ. It is an amazing exchange of our guilt for His righteousness, and our status as fugitives for the freedom we can have as sons and daughters of the King.

- Today's Scripture reading: Psalm 89:11–14; Hebrews 9
- Today's reading from *School of the Prophets*: pages 54–60

Questions to Consider —————————————————

1. What happens when people try to "behave" without having a close, personal relationship with a holy God? Why is that a setup for failure? (See *School of the Prophets* pages 55–56.)

———————————————————————————

———————————————————————————

———————————————————————————

2. In the story I told in today's book reading, what do you think the large bookcase filled with alphabetized volumes of the Book of Fugitives represents? In what way did Jacob represent Christ?

———————————————————————————

———————————————————————————

———————————————————————————

3. Why have our names been crossed out of the Book of Fugitives, so to speak? What did it take to get our names taken off that blacklist?

———————————————————————————

———————————————————————————

———————————————————————————

4. Why is God no longer obligated to punish us for our sin to create justice? (See *School of the Prophets* page 60.) What is it about the foundation of His throne that obligated Him to punish sin in the first place?

———————————————————————————

———————————————————————————

——— DAY 5 ———

VIOLENT GRACE

From the days of John the Baptist until now the kingdom of heaven suffers violence, and violent men take it by force.

Matthew 11:12

Have you ever thought of the cross as a battering ram? That is essentially what it was. The Old Testament Law had set up a wall that the guilty (that would be everyone) could not breach around the Kingdom, and the Old Testament prophets enforced the perimeter of that wall with their judgmental pronouncements. Then Jesus came along and performed a violent act of grace. The cross smashed through the walls of the Kingdom and made a way for all of us to enter in. Our Savior went to war for us and led us in triumph where we could not go ourselves—into victory over death, hell and the grave.

Our Savior also led us into favor, forgiveness and freedom. Look closely at the "Messiah's Mandate" I talk about in today's book reading. The Old Testament version of the mandate ends on a note of judgment, proclaiming "the day of vengeance of our God" (Isaiah 61:2). The New Testament version focuses on a whole new direction, proclaiming "the favorable year of the LORD" (Luke 4:19). That is a profound paradigm shift. Punishment has now given way to forgiveness, and captivity has given way to freedom in Christ.

If, as prophets and prophetesses, we do not follow that shift from old to new, our message is skewed, and it can skew people's perceptions of God. That is why it is so vital to understand the difference between New Testament prophets and Old Testament prophets. The prophets of old had a lot to say about judgment against sinners, but Jesus shifted that paradigm completely. In His violent act of grace at the cross, He showed us that He did not come to judge the world, but to save it.

- Today's Scripture reading: Isaiah 45:2–7; Luke 4:16–21
- Today's reading from *School of the Prophets*: pages 60–64

Questions to Consider _____

1. How is the New Covenant a complete reversal of the former covenant?

   _____

   _____

   _____

2. Why do you think it sounds overly bold to some prophetic people to say that we get to live in a realm of life in which we do not experience judgment?

   _____

   _____

   _____

3. In what way is John 3:16–17 the passage on which all of history pivots? (See *School of the Prophets* page 62.)

   _____

   _____

   _____

4. Were you aware of the custom in synagogues to set up and reserve a Messiah's chair? Describe what you think the reaction of the people must have been when Jesus sat down in it after reading the passage from Isaiah 61 in Nazareth's synagogue.

   _____

   _____

   _____

5. Where has judgment been transferred now that we are no longer the recipients of it? What are the ramifications for us? (See *School of the Prophets* page 64.)

   _____

   _____

   _____

■ Session 2 Life Application _____

In Day 3, question 1 I asked you what choice of direction people who stand at the crossroads of history, the cross, have. Perhaps you answered something like "the choice between accepting or rejecting Jesus Christ as Savior." That would be one correct answer. Or maybe you commented on "the choice between spending eternity in heaven or in hell." That answer works, too. Yet the crossroads at the cross demand of all of us that we make choices that go beyond our salvation. Every day, we go in numerous directions based on what we have done with the cross.

Here is a question I want you to think about carefully: Can a prophet or prophetess take the wrong road there? You can assume that the person has already chosen to believe in Christ's sacrifice and make Him Lord and Savior. But what about beyond that? What are the choices those crossroads present that directly affect someone's prophetic ministry?

I will give you one hint: I am thinking in terms of which direction prophets and prophetesses choose to take their ministry in. Do they choose to go down the road of the Old Covenant, with its pre-cross legalism and judgment? Or do they choose to go down the road of the New Covenant, with its post-cross grace, mercy and ministry of reconciliation?

Think of two or three prophetic people you know (possibly including yourself). Is the choice they made between Old and New at the crossroads obvious in their ministry? How does it affect the way they relate to people (believers and unbelievers)? Would their ministry benefit from them going back to the crossroads and taking a different direction? Would yours?

The thing about the crossroads of history is that we can always retrace our steps, revisit the cross, repent and change direction. In fact, that is what repent means—to change direction. If you need to revisit the cross right now and repent about anything in regard to your prophetic ministry, ask the Holy Spirit to meet you at the crossroads and take you in a new and different direction.

1. The _____ _____ of abortion and the root cause of almost every social dysfunction is the _____ of understanding of the _____ of God.

2. In Matthew 5:44–45, Jesus said, "But I say to you, love your _____ and pray for those who persecute you, so that you may be _____ of your Father who is in heaven; for He causes His sun to rise on the evil and the good, and sends rain on the righteous and the unrighteous." In the Old Covenant, it didn't rain on the _____.

3. God knows the _____ of people, and we _____.

4. Your love for God in the _____ _____ was demonstrated by how much you _____ people who hated God. Jesus lived in the Old Covenant but was _____ in the New one.

5. In a covenant _____, Jesus begins to talk to us about a new way to see the _____ . . . God is extending mercy to people who don't _____ it.

6. I didn't get into the Kingdom through my _____; I got in through _____.

7. It is true that the world deserves to be _____, but God doesn't _____ with us through what we deserve, but through what _____ deserves—and Jesus died for the sins of the world.

8. We live on the _____ side of the _____.

9. How did God _____ the world? He didn't count their _____ against them.

10. The main _____ of an Old Testament prophet was to _____ _____ for sin.

11. You can't do it (keep the Law). That's the whole point of the Old Testament—it's a _____ that leads us to a _____.

12. The _____ of the New Testament prophet has little to do with the _____ of the Old Testament prophet, especially as it pertains to _____.

SESSION 3

TWO DIFFERENT DISPENSATIONS

"The last days" began at the crucifixion of Christ and will end when a new dispensation begins called "the last day," or "Judgment Day." There are thousands of years between "the last days" and "the last day." Many events take place somewhere on "the last days" dispensational timeline. Some of these occurrences are amazing, and some are very troubling. But God's intention for this first dispensation is to pour out His unreasonable, unimaginable, irrefutable, intense love and grace on the entire planet. His goal in this first dispensation is to reconcile the world to Himself by "not counting their trespasses against them" (2 Corinthians 5:19).

School of the Prophets, page 73

— Day 1 —
Taking on a New Role

Now all these things are from God, who reconciled us to Himself through Christ and gave us the ministry of reconciliation, namely, that God was in Christ reconciling the world to Himself, not counting their trespasses against them, and He has committed to us the word of reconciliation.

2 Corinthians 5:18–19

We spent a little time in the previous session looking at how the prophets of old called down the fires of judgment upon the wicked. Warning people about the impending judgment of God was a big part of their role. When Jesus inaugurated the New Covenant of mercy and grace, He did not do away with the role of the prophet; He simply changed it. Under the New Covenant, we prophets and prophetesses have been assigned a new role to play in the coming of the Kingdom.

Taking on a new role can be difficult for us prophetic people, especially since, as we saw in the earlier lessons, we tend to look to the Old Testament prophets as our role models. We also tend to see things in black and white, and we have a strong desire to see justice served. Changing our focus from judgment to reconciliation can be a bit of a challenge for us.

On top of that, part of our new role is to equip the saints for the work of the ministry, to build up the Body of Christ. It has always been easier to tear something down than to build something up. Equipping the saints and building up the Body require more effort on our part than calling down fire and watching things burn.

I asked a "million-dollar question" in today's book reading: "What would happen if you took an Old Testament prophet and transferred him to the New Testament side of the cross?" We saw the answer to that in Elijah. But the flip side of that question is also worth contemplating: "What would happen if you took a New Testament prophet and transferred him to the Old Testament side of the cross?"

Unfortunately, we see the answer to that in many of today's prophets and prophetesses who refuse to take on their new role as ministers of reconciliation and builders of the Body. They are still busily engaging in a ministry of judgment that is a far cry from the role God has assigned us in this New Covenant. A revelation of their new role could transform their ministry! I hope the lessons ahead will play a part in helping bring forth that revelation.

- Today's Scripture reading: Ephesians 4:1–16
- Today's reading from *School of the Prophets*: pages 65–67

Questions to Consider _____

1. It would be hard to find two roles more completely different than the ministry of judgment, in which you call down fire on sinners, and the ministry of reconciliation, in which you do not count people's trespasses against them. If you are a prophetic person, have you struggled with choosing between these two roles? Are you beginning to understand through this study more about which role we are called to play under the New Covenant and why?

_____

_____

_____

2. What two things about the prophets does Ephesians 4:11–13 highlight for us? (See *School of the Prophets* page 66.) Why are those two things so vital for us to know?

_____

_____

_____

3. Why might "not counting people's trespasses against them" destroy the ministry of a few of the prophets and prophetesses of our time? What things might they need to learn about the role they are to play this side of the cross?

_____

_____

_____

—— Day 2 ——

Exception or Rule?

And as he heard these words, Ananias fell down and breathed his last; and great fear came over all who heard of it.

Acts 5:5

The death of Ananias and his wife, Sapphira, undoubtedly took the early Church in Acts 5 by surprise. In fact, I think it took the apostle Peter by surprise as well. Ananias and Sapphira surely were not the only believers who had ever lied to their leaders, and they probably were not the only ones who got caught. As we have already seen, mercy was the new rule of the New Covenant, yet for some reason God made the two of them an exception to the rule.

God can take home whomever He pleases whenever He pleases and do such things for whatever reason He chooses. When He chooses to make an exception to a rule, as He did with Ananias and Sapphira, that does not mean we are justified in taking that single exception and making a culture out of it. If God had intended the Church to establish a culture in which every lie resulted in a death at the feet of Church leadership, the survival rate among believers would have been pretty small—and still would be today.

God had His reasons for including the shocking story in Acts 5 as part of Scripture, and I agree that it seems more like an Old Covenant judgment in the midst of the New. But there were also New Testament mercies in the midst of the Old. Think of Rahab, the Gentile prostitute. Under Old Testament norms, that kind of woman would have been dispatched quickly and mercilessly as the Israelites conquered the Promised Land. Yet she was promised life and became an exception to the rule.

God can make such exceptions because He is God, and we need to leave them in His hands. If we would do that, there would not be so many attempts (today and throughout Church history) to take biblical exceptions and make rules out of them. I tell you in today's reading about the "prophetic round-table" I attended where the discussion was all about "bringing back the days of Ananias and Sapphira." Why would so many prophets and prophetesses jump on that bandwagon when it is not even a scriptural pattern? I think it is because, as I said in yesterday's lesson, it is way easier to call down fire on people than to work at building up the Church. Let's be the exception to that rule, though, and not take the easy road.

- Today's Scripture reading: Acts 5:1–11
- Today's reading from *School of the Prophets*: pages 67–70

Questions to Consider —————————————————————

1. Have you been in discussions like the ones I have at Bethel School of the Prophets where the case of Ananias and Sapphira is a hot topic of debate? What are some of the conclusions you have heard people arrive at to explain it?

————————————————————————

————————————————————————

————————————————————————

2. Why do you think Ananias and Sapphira were made an exception to the rule? Do you believe, as I do, that they are still in heaven, not hell?

————————————————————————

————————————————————————

————————————————————————

3. What are some of the dangers in Church leaders taking an exception in the Scripture and making an entire culture out of it? Give some examples of the negative results you have seen when that kind of error happens.

————————————————————————

————————————————————————

————————————————————————

4. In what way does the story of Ananias and Sapphira powerfully illustrate the incredible mercy of God? (See *School of the Prophets* page 69.)

————————————————————————

————————————————————————

————————————————————————

— Day 3 —

The Last Days

"And it shall be in the last days," God says, "that I will pour forth of My Spirit on all mankind; and your sons and your daughters shall prophesy, and your young men shall see visions, and your old men shall dream dreams; even on My bondslaves, both men and women, I will in those days pour forth of My Spirit and they shall prophesy."

Acts 2:17–18

Now that we have looked closely at the two covenants, Old and New, I want to look closely at two dispensations that are contained in the New Covenant. These dispensations are "the last days" and "the last day."

Do you see the difference between them? Only one little *s* on the end, and yet that small difference contains vitally important distinctions. We must understand the distinctions between these dispensations if we are to avoid becoming seriously dysfunctional as prophets and prophetesses.

Today we will look at "the last days" with an *s*, and in tomorrow's lesson I will cover "the last day." Peter refers to the last days in Acts 2 when he is quoting the book of Joel, and we are living now in the last days that Peter and the prophet Joel were talking about. These last days began at the cross and will continue until Judgment Day (the last day).

God has one major intention during this first dispensation of the last days—to pour out His love, grace, favor and mercy on the entire planet and reconcile the world to Himself. To that end, two manifestations mark these days: God will pour our His Spirit on all mankind, and all who call on the name of the Lord will be saved.

What glorious days we live in, days of mercy, not judgment! The question for us to consider is this: Does the way we conduct our prophetic ministry reflect that glory?

- Today's Scripture reading: Acts 2
- Today's reading from *School of the Prophets*: pages 70–73

Questions to Consider _____

    1. Why do you suppose the last days dispensation is also called the "great and glorious day of the Lord"?

    2. Metaphorically speaking, what do the sun and moon represent in the passage from Acts 2 that I talk about in today's reading? What dispensation began when the sun turned dark and the moon turned to blood? (See *School of the Prophets* page 72.)

    3. What is glorious about the two manifestations that mark the dispensation we are now living in? (See *School of the Prophets* page 73.)

    4. How much time elapses between "the last days" and "the last day"? When will we change from one dispensation to the other? (See *School of the Prophets* page 73.)

DAY 4

THE LAST DAY

> God is now declaring to men that all people everywhere should
> repent, because He has fixed a day in which He will judge the
> world in righteousness.
>
> Acts 17:30–31

Those of us who burn for justice will see its day come in the second dispensation I want to look at, "the last day." Judgment Day will arrive, and God will judge the world in righteousness, turning His spotlight on the hearts of all men.

Today is not yet that day, although many prophetic people act as if that last day is already here. They forget the difference in the two dispensations we are talking about, which is why Paul had to remind us in 1 Corinthians 4:5, "Do not go on passing judgment before the time, but wait until the Lord comes." Such prophets try to impose a coming dispensation (the last day) on their prophetic role in the current times (the last days), thereby rendering their prophetic ministry ineffective.

Imposing the coming dispensation on your prophetic ministry is no better than imposing the former Old Covenant on it—and notice that both of those, past and future, focus on *judgment*. So many prophets long to impose judgment on peoples and nations, and if you challenge them, they will fight passionately for their right to punish people. But meting out punishment is not our responsibility. God has commissioned us to extend the Kingdom wherever we go and carry the news of a heavenly Father who loves and desires a relationship with every person He has created.

True prophetic ministry in our day has no place for angry people looking for a place to vent their rage. We would do well as prophets and prophetesses to remember that "the anger of man does not achieve the righteousness of God" (James 1:20). Again, ours is the ministry of reconciliation. It is so important for us to understand the times we live in, as the sons of Issachar did in their day, and to know how we should act. Part of that understanding comes in knowing the difference between the two dispensations that mark the New Covenant.

- Today's Scripture reading: 1 Chronicles 12:32; 2 Peter 3:7–15
- Today's reading from *School of the Prophets*: pages 73–77

Questions to Consider _____

1. Have you ever met someone (prophetic or otherwise) who just seems passionate about seeing other people get what they deserve? What is it that is so disturbing about that?

2. Paul stated in 1 Corinthians 4:4, "For I am conscious of nothing against myself, yet I am not by this acquitted; but the one who examines me is the Lord." What ramifications do you think that statement has on our prophetic ministry? (See *School of the Prophets* page 74.)

3. What do you think it means to say "whatever you misunderstand, you will mistreat"? In what ways so far is this *School of the Prophets* study helping you avoid mistreating your prophetic commission?

4. Why is it incumbent upon us as God's prophets and prophetesses to use our gifts to find the gold buried in the dirt of people's lives? Why wouldn't it be more effective for us to concentrate on finding and exposing all the sin in the lives of sinners?

—— DAY 5 ——
DAMAGE CONTROL

Love never fails.
1 Corinthians 13:8

Even if the prophetic words you deliver are 100 percent accurate 100 percent of the time, they can still be wrong. What do I mean? They can be given in the wrong spirit or in the wrong tone, causing offense in people's lives and undermining your relationship with them.

I can tell you from painful experience that if you make it your prophetic practice to call out people's sins, speak negatively to them and embarrass them in public with what should be private pronouncements, you will do more harm than good. I relate some of my hard-learned lessons along those lines in today's reading from *School of the Prophets*.

It took what I call a "revelation bump" to get me moving in the right direction, from being a prophet of judgment to becoming a prophet of mercy. It took me a while to understand that my prophetic commission should be rooted in love. It also took some serious damage control on my part to make up for what had been years of harsh prophetic deliveries.

In prophetic ministry, love is the key to damage control. There is a reason why we find the "love chapter" of the Bible, 1 Corinthians 13, sandwiched between the main chapters on the gifts of the Spirit. Like every other gift of the Spirit, prophecy is one of the love languages of God. When people witness you moving in the prophetic, are they seeing and hearing the language of love? They should be.

- Today's Scripture reading: 1 Corinthians 13
- Today's reading from *School of the Prophets*: pages 77–78

Questions to Consider _____

1. Have you ever thought of the prophetic ministry as being rooted in love? Why or why not?

   _____

   _____

   _____

2. Describe a "revelation bump" that you have run into in your spiritual growth process (whether it involved prophetic ministry or something else). How did it jar you into reevaluating your behavior?

   _____

   _____

   _____

3. Without compromising the accuracy of their words, what are some ways prophets and prophetesses can tone down harsh deliveries and turn up love?

   _____

   _____

   _____

▪ Session 3 Life Application

In this session's reading from *School of the Prophets* and in Day 4, question 2 I quoted Paul's statement that "the one who examines me is the Lord" (1 Corinthians 4:4). Take some time right now to invite the Lord to examine your heart in regard to the things we have covered in this session. For example,

- Ask Him if you have the kind of understanding you need about the difference between the two dispensations of "the last days" and "the last day."
- Ask Him if you need more enlightenment on those, or on the different roles prophets played under the Old and New Covenants (which we talked about in Session 2).
- Ask Him to show you what adjustments you need to make in your role.
- Also ask Him to reveal any scriptural exceptions to the rule that you have wanted to help make into a culture in the Church, which is damaging.
- Ask Him if your prophetic ministry (or whatever ministry you are called to) is rooted deeply enough in love.
- Finally, ask Him to help you apply His answers to your life and ministry so that you can do a better job equipping the saints for the ministry and building the Body of Christ.

Asking the Lord to examine you in these areas and putting His responses into practice will help you grow in your office. In addition, you may also want to consider getting some feedback about these areas from the leaders in your life. Their responses will help you grow, too. How would your leaders answer these same questions about you that you asked God? Ask them!

■ Session 3 Video Guide _____

1. Your _____ (as a prophet or prophetess) is to find the _____ in the dirt of a person's life.

2. You don't have to be prophetic to find _____ in sinners' lives, and you don't have to be prophetic to find _____ in the people you live with, but you have to be prophetic to find _____ in some people's lives.

3. God said, "Over My _____ _____ will you go to hell," but there are people who _____ over His dead body and they _____ hell.

4. God never _____ _____ choice, because _____ requires _____.

5. There is a difference between the _____ _____ and the _____ _____.

6. The last day is a day of _____, and we are _____ the judge.

7. There is a day of judgment, but there are _____ _____ when God will pour His _____ out on all _____.

8. Those are _____ and _____ days, and everyone who calls on the name of the Lord in those days will be _____.

9. We live in the last days, NOT the last day, and so our ministry is still the ministry of _____, and not _____.

10. Between the _____ day of the Lord and the day of _____ of our God (Judgment Day) are _____ of years.

11. A lot of people bring _____ _____ into the last days and end up with a very _____ prophetic ministry.

PROPHETIC
PERSPECTIVES

Intellectual agreement with biblical concepts is the beginning of developing the right core values, yet until we work them out and walk them out in our lives, they remain philosophies or good ideas. For Kingdom core values to direct our lives as prophets and prophetesses, they must become our identity—who we are and *how* we think. Yes, it is true that core values determine *what* we think. But more importantly, they are the lenses through which we view the *what* in life, and subsequently they determine *how* we behave. There is no such thing as core values that do not affect our behavior.

School of the Prophets, pages 109–110

DAY 1

SEEING CLEARLY

Keep your heart with all diligence, for out of it spring the issues of life.

Proverbs 4:23 NKJV

If you have ever worn glasses or contact lenses, you know how vital it is to have the right prescription so that you can see clearly. If your lenses are just a little bit off, a little scratched or defective, you will wind up viewing a distorted image of the world around you, and it will throw off your perception.

In a sense, the same thing is true in prophetic ministry. Prophets were referred to as "seers" in the Old Testament, and seeing clearly is what a lot of this study is about. Seers cannot see clearly, though, if the lenses of their core values are damaged or off, even just a little bit. Our core values are the lenses that determine the way we see life. A slight distortion in our lenses can have huge ramifications on our prophecies.

Different prophets do see things differently (yes, there are different prophetic personalities), and that is not an issue. We each have a prophetic accent, only instead of an accent on our speech, it is an accent on our sight. We see things through the filters of our experiences, ethnic origins and the like. I believe God factors in our prophetic "accent" when He uses us to speak a word, so that the unique flavor of our life flavors the words we give. (That is not the same as adding to what God says, which is a different issue entirely.) It is all right for me to see through different filters than you, so long as our core-value lenses are not damaged. As long as the Kingdom core values beneath our "accents" are foundationally solid, our perceptions will be unique from each other, but not distorted.

How do we keep our lenses in good working order, so to speak? We renew our minds so that we have the mind of Christ. We filter everything we see through the mind of Christ, which acts like our optic nerve to turn our skewed perspectives right side up. To put it in aeronautical terms, it is a matter of piloting our way through the "spatial disorientation" this world can cause and using our gauges to discern reality from virtual reality. Pilots have been known to fly upside down and point their planes toward the ground when they rely on gut instinct in a storm. You can imagine the results of doing that! As prophets and prophetesses, we can have a tendency to rely on gut instinct, too, but we must trust our instruments to direct our lives and ministries. Our gauges are Kingdom core values.

In the rest of this session, we will be looking at the importance of our core values, particularly how to define, assess and assimilate them so that we can see clearly no matter what the spiritual weather. Think of this session as spiritual flight school.

- Today's Scripture reading: 1 Samuel 9:5–14
- Today's reading from *School of the Prophets*: pages 79–85

Questions to Consider _____

1. How is prophesying through our unique visual accents different than adding to a prophetic word the Lord has given us? (See *School of the Prophets* pages 80–81.)

_____

_____

_____

2. As seers, why must prophets and prophetesses question how they see things? Why is it so important to avoid viewing things through a bad or damaged lens? (See *School of the Prophets* page 81.)

_____

_____

_____

3. I told you the story in today's book reading of the prejudiced translator I was given in a crusade, who completely twisted my message of freedom into a message of bondage. How can faulty core values act like a bad translator when it comes to our spiritual perceptions?

_____

_____

_____

4. When we have pain and brokenness in our hearts, what can they do to our prophetic insight and foresight? What was King Solomon's solution to that? (See *School of the Prophets* pages 83–84.)

_____

_____

_____

5. Would you rather be in a plane in which the pilot was trusting his instruments or his gut instincts? How does piloting passengers safely compare to the prophetic ministry?

_____

_____

_____

— DAY 2 —

ENLIGHTENED EYES

I pray that the eyes of your heart may be enlightened.

Ephesians 1:18

Building with light. That is how I like to think of the prophetic ministry. Jesus is the Light of the world, and He enlightens us about who God is, who we are in Him and what we can accomplish for the Kingdom. Then He tells us that *we* are the light of the world, so we take what He has revealed to us and we enlighten others with it. It is an amazing process that more and more brightly shines a light on the goodness of God.

Certain things are necessary for that process of passing the light to stay bright. In order to shine on others, we prophets and prophetesses have to be seeing clearly with the eyes of our hearts. Our worldview has to be rooted in the eternal realities of the Kingdom, from which we form our foundational core values.

When our core values are rooted in the Kingdom and in who God really is, it perpetuates healthy ecosystems and wholesome prophetic communities. When our core values are faulty or damaged, however, it perpetuates dysfunction. If there is anything we believers are good at, it is spiritualizing our dysfunctions! An angry person will see God through the scratched lens of anger and think He is an angry God, which will have all kinds of ramifications on that person's prophetic ministry. (That is the case with many of the "Prophets of Doom" I have run into.) A person looking through the clear lenses of Kingdom core values will see God as loving, affectionate and good, which will also have all kinds of ramifications on his or her prophetic ministry.

There is nothing like clear, sharp, focused vision to bring health to your prophetic ministry. The pure in heart will see God, Jesus told us in Matthew 5:8. They will also see each other more clearly. No log jams will get in their way in their own eyes as they reach out to help take the speck out of their brothers' and sisters' eyes. Isn't that one of the things we prophets are called to do, help extract logs from the hearts of the hurting? I think so, but it takes enlightened eyes to do so. And the only way to have the clear lenses of Kingdom core values to see through is for our hearts to be enlightened by the King.

- Today's Scripture reading: Matthew 5:1–11; Ephesians 1
- Today's reading from *School of the Prophets*: pages 85–90

Questions to Consider _____

1. How is the way we view others one of the main ways we can discern if we have a log in our own eye? (See *School of the Prophets* page 86.)

_____

_____

_____

2. What are three primary themes upon which our core values need to be founded? (See *School of the Prophets* page 87.)

_____

_____

_____

3. Name two or three the ways that angry scratches on someone's "lenses" will affect that person's hearing and ultimately his or her ministry. (See *School of the Prophets* page 88.) Can you think of any other ways besides those I listed in today's book reading?

_____

_____

_____

4. What does it mean to say that who God is *to us*, He will be *through us*?

_____

_____

_____

5. Name two or three ways in which having Kingdom core values manifests in a person's prophetic ministry. (See *School of the Prophets* pages 89–90.) Can you think of any other ways besides those I listed?

_____

_____

_____

DAY 3
DEFINING THE ESSENTIALS

Pursue love, yet desire earnestly spiritual gifts, but especially that you may prophesy. . . . One who prophesies speaks to men for edification and exhortation and consolation. One who speaks in a tongue edifies himself; but one who prophesies edifies the church.

1 Corinthians 14:1, 3–4

Developing Kingdom core values the right way requires three things. Today we will cover the first thing, *defining* what healthy core values are. Then in Days 4 and 5 of this session, we will cover the other two things, *assessing* our current core values and *assimilating* healthy ones.

Definitions are important, which is why we will start there. Webster tells us that a definition is a statement expressing the *essential nature* of something. In today's reading from *School of the Prophets*, I give you several examples of Kingdom core values that are essential for us to have as prophets and prophetesses. I will not relist them all here, since in a few moments you will get to them in the book. I do want you to notice, though, that for each core value I list, I also tell you what it teaches us or trains us to do in regard to the prophetic ministry.

A list of definitions can be of some use in our study of this topic, but without taking what we learn and applying it to our lives, all the definitions we study will be nothing more than words on a page. That is why doing the life application exercise in each of these workbook sessions is so important. You and I can study spiritual principles and foundational Scriptures until the Lord returns, but in order to accomplish what God has called us to, we also have to *apply* them. You have no doubt heard the phrase before that we Christians need to "walk the talk," and doing that is absolutely essential for those of us who are in the prophetic ministry.

- Today's Scripture reading: 1 Corinthians 14:1–33
- Today's reading from *School of the Prophets*: pages 90–95

Questions to Consider _____

1. Have you ever met a Christian (without naming any names) who was really good at studying the things of the Kingdom and talking the talk, but who was a little slow on the application? What did that do to the person's credibility as a witness for Christ? What might it do to someone's prophetic ministry?

_____

_____

_____

2. How does it help us to specifically define the healthy Kingdom core values that we should carry into our prophetic ministry? How are these core values also applicable to other ministries and to believers in general?

_____

_____

_____

3. Of the core values I listed and defined, which one hit home the hardest with you? Why do you think that one stood out to you the most?

_____

_____

_____

— DAY 4 —
PUT TO THE TEST

Examine me, O LORD, and try me; test my mind and my heart.

Psalm 26:2

Today's lesson will put you to the test. The reading from *School of the Prophets* includes an assessment test for you to take, and it is important that you do not skip class because it is a test day! This test is important to take because in order to develop solid Kingdom core values, you need to assess and analyze the core values you currently have. Assessing your current core values and measuring them against the truth will go a long way toward making sure any scratches or defects in the lenses through which you "see" are corrected, so that you have a clear perspective from which to minister prophetically.

Do not worry; you cannot fail this test. It is not a pass/fail kind of test. It is more subjective, and a high positive score does not qualify you as a bona fide prophet or prophetess any more than a low score disqualifies you from the prophetic ministry. It does not work that way. Whenever I teach on core values, people ask me if there is some way they can determine whether the lenses of their life are clear or distorted, so I developed this test as a tool to help you determine that. It will help you gauge how your current core values most likely are affecting you as a person and as a prophet or prophetess.

Base your answers to this test on the way you are *most often*, not the way you are on your best or worst days. (And do not base your answers on what you think the "right" answer should be—there are no right answers.) Then add up your score according to the directions in the book so that you know what your final grade is. Analyze your final score according to the guidelines I provide after the test.

If you end up in the extremes of a high or low on the score graph, do not feel as if you must either rejoice or despair. Simply take my comments about extreme scores to heart and decide what steps you can take to bring some balance where needed. More likely, you will land somewhere in a mid-range score on the positive or negative side. From there, you can start looking for themes that will help reveal overall patterns in your way of thinking and "seeing." The Holy Spirit will assist you in analyzing your score results and will guide you in arriving at a clearer view of life. A wise, godly counselor may also be of some help where needed.

Once you have been put to the test, tomorrow's lesson on assimilating healthy Kingdom core values will help you adjust your lens prescription even more precisely so that you can fulfill God's call on you as a seer with grace and truth.

- Today's Scripture reading: 1 Kings 19; Psalm 139:23–24; 2 Corinthians 13:5–9
- Today's reading from *School of the Prophets*: pages 95–104

Questions to Consider _____

1. What was your score on today's Core Values Assessment Test? Based on my comments in the book about analyzing your final score, what are a couple main things the test told you about yourself? Were there patterns in your thinking that the test brought to light?

   _____

   _____

   _____

2. In what ways might the things the test revealed to you about yourself affect your ministry as a prophet or prophetess? (Or how do they affect your ministry doing whatever God has called you to, if it does not involve the office of a prophet? Our core values affect every area of our lives.)

   _____

   _____

   _____

3. Did it surprise you that a +200 (positive 200) on the test would not necessarily be a perfect score? What do you think the difference is between having a Big Sugar Daddy perspective of God and having a positive perspective balanced by a paradigm for what I called the Lion side of the Son of God? (See *School of the Prophets* pages 102–103.)

   _____

   _____

   _____

4. I also mentioned briefly in today's book reading that prophets and prophetesses can have their perspectives tainted by spiritual warfare, as Elijah once did. In what ways do you feel such warfare has been a factor for you as you work to fulfill your divine purposes? (If the Holy Spirit has shown you any bondages you need to get free of in order to more effectively develop Kingdom core values and minister to others, make sure you follow through on finding freedom.)

_____

_____

_____

— DAY 5 —

HEART VERSUS HEAD

... that Christ may dwell in your hearts through faith; and that
you, being rooted and grounded in love, may be able to comprehend
with all the saints what is the breadth and length and height and
depth, and to know the love of Christ which surpasses knowledge,
that you may be filled up to all the fullness of God.

Ephesians 3:17–19

Now that we have defined some healthy core values in Day 3 and assessed our personal core values in Day 4, today I want to look at the third thing we need to do to make sure we are seeing life clearly. We need to *assimilate* Kingdom core values into our hearts so that they become the lenses through which we live and minister.

It is one thing to talk about and define Kingdom core values and to assess the values we currently hold, but it can be quite another thing to assimilate the right core values and walk them out in our lives. (We talked a little about that in Day 3.) Even if we have good head knowledge about core values and all that they involve and affect, what it really boils down to is our hearts.

Our heart is the throne of our core values, not our head. It is one thing to know about something and another thing to do it or apply it. That is where some more of those "revelation bumps" I told you about come in for us. In fact, I tell you two more of my revelation bump stories in today's reading. (My spiritual growth has definitely been a bumpy road at times.)

Being exposed to spiritual truths like core values as an academic exercise is a great start, and intellectually agreeing with them is even better. Yet for all that, they remain just philosophies or good ideas in us until we work them out and walk them out in our lives. That is what it means to assimilate Kingdom core values—to work them out and walk them out in our everyday lives and ministries. And that is how Kingdom core values become our identity, part of who we are and how we think and act. They move from our heads to our hearts.

- Today's Scripture reading: Ephesians 3:14–21; James 1:22–27
- Today's reading from *School of the Prophets*: pages 104–110

Questions to Consider _____

1. What does it show in us when there is a disconnection between what we say we believe and the way we actually behave? What does it take to solve that kind of disconnection? (See *School of the Prophets* page 104.)

_____

_____

_____

2. I described to you in today's reading why it is difficult for a "pauper" like I was to become a king. Have you ever struggled with the pauper syndrome spiritually, emotionally or otherwise? In what ways did it affect you, and in what ways did you affect others because of it? What happened (or needs to happen) to resolve it?

_____

_____

_____

3. Why is there no such thing as core values that do not affect our behavior? (See *School of the Prophets* pages 109–110.)

_____

_____

_____

4. How does our assimilation of healthy Kingdom core values help us as prophets and prophetesses minister truth and freedom to others? (See *School of the Prophets* page 110.)

_____

_____

_____

■ Session 4 Life Application ─────────────

Remember my comment in the book that there cannot be change in us until we have a revelation and "see" that something is not right? Admitting we have a problem really is the first step, and it is a healthy one. Take that step now by picking three or four core values off my list of definitions in the book that you felt were new or deeper revelation to you. In other words, by reading the definitions, you realized you might lack those particular core values and need to assimilate them.

Trust me, you do not want to go about this the hard way. Do you also remember my stories of how adversity introduced me to myself and forced me to take a look at some of the faulty core values I held? It is easier to read the definitions, take the assessment test, admit any problems up front and work toward correcting them. Toward that end, did your assessment test in Day 4 show any patterns in your thinking that might have been affected by a deficiency in the core values you chose? How might you replace your damaged core values with healthy ones off the list? I suggested one way in the book—by asking ourselves how each core value makes us behave in the Kingdom. We need to determine what our subsequent behavior will look like once we assimilate a certain core value, and then walk it out.

If you are struggling with working through this application yourself, you could sit down with a trusted Christian counselor or friend and go over the list of definitions and your score on the Core Values Assessment Test. Using those two things as tools, you could determine together two or three core values that you need to work on assimilating, and you could determine a course of action toward that goal.

Another approach you could take is to have two or three close friends take the Core Values Assessment Test for you—as they "perceive" that you would answer it—and then give you feedback anywhere their perceptions of you were different than your perception of yourself.

If you will take whatever time and steps are necessary to align your core values with Kingdom core values, the resulting increase in your effectiveness both in life and ministry will be worth the effort.

■ **Session 4 Video Guide** _____

1. You see, hear and perceive the world with an _____.

2. You _____ the world not as it is, but as _____ are.

3. Core values are the _____ of your life . . . core values are the way you _____ life.

4. When a prophet says God is _____, it's pretty difficult not to have _____ words.

5. The way I see God _____ the way I do _____.

6. If I believe God is loving, then I believe the _____ about people. I extend _____ to people; I look for _____ in people.

7. God is love, and _____ love casts out fear because fear involves _____. Therefore, _____ _____ should flow out of love, not out of fear.

8. When I prophesy and it creates fear and anxiety, I have _____ with the _____ spirit.

9. It takes the _____ of God AND the _____ of God to equal _____ (truth).

10. When people _____ our prophetic gift, they should _____ God's _____.

SESSION 5

PROPHECY VERSUS PROPHETS

The Gift of Prophecy	The Office of Prophet/Prophetess
It is a gift of the Holy Spirit.	It is a gift of Christ.
It is something you do.	It is something you are.
Every believer is exhorted to seek to prophesy.	God chooses prophets; it is not our choice.
It is for edification, exhortation and comfort.	It is to direct, correct, warn, govern and equip.
Prophetic ability is the gift.	The prophet himself (or herself) is a gift.
The person is classified as a saint.	The person is called as part of the fivefold team.
The gift is for life.	The calling is for life.

School of the Prophets, page 123

── DAY 1 ──

IT'S A GIFT

One who prophesies speaks to men for edification and exhortation and consolation.

1 Corinthians 14:3

One of my main goals in putting together this study was to clear up any confusion between the *office* of the prophet or prophetess and the *gift* of prophecy. There is a world of difference between the two, and confusing them causes a lot of issues in the Church. Just because someone gives accurate prophetic words, that does not mean he or she holds the office of a prophet/prophetess. A prophetic word can come through any believer operating in the gift of prophecy. It is one of the nine spiritual gifts 1 Corinthians 12 talks about. Every believer is urged to pursue these gifts, especially the gift of prophecy.

The office of the prophet/prophetess is something different, and we will look specifically at the office in Day 3 of this session. Let's focus here on the gift, though, and its purposes. The gift is given not to correct, but to encourage the Church. The overall tone of a prophetic word that comes through this gift will be positive; it will edify, exhort and encourage those who hear it. Its goal is to bring out the best in people. Rather than condemning them, it often will direct them toward answers to their struggles with sin.

Because it is a gift, the receiver does not receive it based on any merit of his or her own. Sometimes those who are immature in their faith operate in this gift. Sometimes young children operate in it. We train everyone at Bethel, young and old physically and spiritually, to seek the spiritual gifts, including the gift of prophecy. So again, if someone gives a prophetic word, that does not necessarily validate the person's walk with the Lord, nor does it automatically install the person in the office of a prophet/prophetess. It simply means that he or she is operating in the gift of prophecy, which is a good thing.

- Today's Scripture reading: Galatians 5:16–25
- Today's reading from *School of the Prophets*: pages 111–115

Questions to Consider _____

1. Did you realize before now that when it comes to prophecy, the *office* and the *gift* are two different things? Did you realize that even if you are not called to the office of a prophet/prophetess, you can and should seek to operate in the gift of prophecy?

2. Why do you think that children are sometimes more uninhibited and more powerfully prophetic than adults are? Have you seen that in evidence in your church setting? What could you do to encourage it?

3. How does a critical, condemning word that sets a negative tone violate the primary purpose of the gift of prophecy? (See *School of the Prophets* page 114.)

4. What does it mean to say that we should prophesy an answer to someone rather than prophesying a problem? How does this release grace to break bondages? (See *School of the Prophets* page 114.)

— DAY 2 —

RECEPTION VERSUS PERCEPTION

Do not quench the Spirit; do not despise prophetic utterances.
But examine everything carefully; hold fast to that which is good.

1 Thessalonians 5:19–21

Before we move on to talk about the office of the prophet or prophetess as compared to the gift of prophecy, let's take today to talk about another important comparison—the way prophetic insight was *received* in the Old Testament, compared to how it is *perceived* in the New Testament.

Because the Holy Spirit did not live inside people during Old Testament times, as He does today, they were not temples of the Holy Spirit in the same way as we are. Consequently, when the Holy Spirit came upon a prophet and he received a word and prophesied, it was a big deal. And the people hearing that word did not have the same ability to judge it as we do, so their method of checking a prophetic word for accuracy was simply the "wait and see" method—waiting to see if it came to pass.

You and I, however, are what I call in today's book reading a holy house for two. Both your spirit and the Holy Spirit live inside you, so you can perceive a word in your spirit that is from the Holy Spirit. Both of you are involved, which is why we have the responsibility to judge prophetic words that come forth.

It is important to discern the source of a word—whether it is from God's Spirit, the person's spirit or a demonic spirit. As well-intentioned as people may be, sometimes in their zeal they can represent a good idea coming just from themselves as a God idea. Sometimes they can also get part of a word right and part of it wrong, which I talk about more in today's reading. These are some things we need to take into consideration as we judge a prophetic word, and then we can "eat the meat and spit out the bones."

- Today's Scripture reading: 2 Peter 1:1–8; 1 Corinthians 14:29–33
- Today's reading from *School of the Prophets*: pages 115–118

Questions to Consider _____

1. Why is it that as New Testament believers, we process prophetic revelation from a completely different perspective than people did in Old Testament times? (See *School of the Prophets* page 115.)

_____

_____

_____

2. What does it mean to say that each of us is a holy house for two? How does this enable us to perceive prophetic words?

_____

_____

_____

3. In the Old Testament, what did prophets judge? What are prophets told to judge in the New Testament? (See *School of the Prophets* page 117.)

_____

_____

_____

4. What are the three parts that make up prophecy? How does that explain why part of a prophetic word can be right and part can be wrong? (See *School of the Prophets* page 118.)

_____

_____

_____

— DAY 3 —

CALLED TO THE OFFICE

The gifts and the calling of God are irrevocable.

Romans 11:29

When someone is called to the office of a prophet or prophetess, that person *is* the gift. It goes beyond having the gift or ability to prophesy. As we saw in Day 1 of this session, any believer can operate in that gift. But to *be* the gift is why the office differs from the gift itself. The gifts Christ gave the Church as listed in Ephesians 4:11 are other people (the fivefold ministers), among them prophets. It is not so much about what they do as who they are.

The three components of any mature ministry are someone's gifting, calling and anointing. Each of these components relates differently to the gift of prophecy and the office of a prophet. In today's *School of the Prophets* reading, I describe for you just how. I also describe some things to watch out for, lest they give rise to a dysfunctional ministry. For example, adopting a performance-based identity in which you need to prophesy over everyone and everything as a way to validate yourself creates dysfunction. Misunderstanding the way you see, hear and "feel" multidimensionally as a prophet or prophetess can make you feel crazy. Neglecting the necessity of abiding in relationship with God can diminish your anointing.

Whether you are called to the office or operate in the gift, there are so many things to learn about prophecy and how to increase your effectiveness in it. We will continue looking at many of those things in the sessions ahead, especially those things that help establish a healthy prophetic community. In today's lesson, however, I want you to take special note of the chart I provide on page 123 of the book. It summarizes the difference between the *gift* of prophecy and being called to the *office*. Whichever side of the chart you fall on, comprehending the difference will make you an even more valuable part of your prophetic community. Your effectiveness for the Kingdom will increase because God will be able to work through you in exactly the way He intended so that you will accomplish the divine purpose He has in mind just for you.

- Today's Scripture reading: 1 Peter 4:7–11; 1 John 4
- Today's reading from *School of the Prophets*: pages 118–123

Questions to Consider _____

1. When it comes to the prophetic, what is the difference between having the gift and being the gift?

   _____

   _____

   _____

2. What kind of dysfunction in ministry flows out of a performance-based identity? How can a believer overcome this unhealthy dynamic? (See *School of the Prophets* pages 119–120.)

   _____

   _____

   _____

3. When is a person called to the office of a prophet or prophetess? Name a few of the ways in which this particular call might affect someone. (See *School of the Prophets* pages 120–121.)

   _____

   _____

   _____

4. What is the anointing always associated with? What single factor most affects the ebb and flow of the anointing on a person? (See *School of the Prophets* pages 121–122.)

   _____

   _____

   _____

5. At present, which side of the gift-versus-office summary chart do you fall on? What differences between the two sides has the chart clarified for you? How will this help you in your life and/or ministry?

— DAY 4 —

CRISIS INTERVENTION

Every good thing given and every perfect gift is from above, coming
down from the Father of lights, with whom there is no variation
or shifting shadow.

James 1:17

Every good thing comes to us from our Father. Every bad thing does
not. You would think that would be obvious, but it is not, not even to
believers. For example, many of us operate—and we prophesy—from
a core value that God causes all natural disasters. Even the secular world
backs this up. Think about how the insurance industry uses the term *acts of
God* for natural disasters. That teaches unbelievers to blame everything bad
on God, which is a faulty and damaging core value from which to live life.

Yes, God created the laws of nature, but they can and do perpetuate without His intervention. It is crucial for us to understand this as His children
who represent Him and His character to the lost. And it is so important for
modern-day prophets and prophetesses to know the difference between giving a warning and pronouncing judgment. The two show very different sides
of the character of God. We have already seen how in Old Testament times,
over and over prophets proclaimed judgment in the form of some looming
natural disaster about to come upon a people or a nation as punishment for
their sins. That was part of their role, but it is no longer the role of New
Covenant prophets. We now have the ministry of reconciliation.

The prophets and prophetesses of today do prophesy words of warning
(not judgment) about coming natural disasters, but they do so as a means
of crisis intervention. Their goal is to divert a crisis or save people from its

consequences. I give you an amazing example of that from Guatemala in today's book reading. The prophetic warnings of today are not meant to descend upon the lost as judgments, although the "Prophets of Doom" I have talked about tend to twist them around in that direction. The prophetic warnings of today are crisis interventions sent through the goodness and mercy of God to save and protect people.

- Today's Scripture reading: 2 Timothy 4:1–8
- Today's reading from *School of the Prophets*: pages 123–128

Questions to Consider _____

1. Why is it that those who hold a prophetic office are sometimes called upon in our day to prophesy warnings and corrections, but those with the gift of prophecy are not, due to the purpose of that gift? (See *School of the Prophets* pages 123–124.)

2. The seasoned prophet Agabus did not call for repentance when he prophesied a coming famine in Acts because he did not relate the famine to judgment for sin. In the form of crisis intervention, what was the response of those who heard the word Agabus gave? (See Acts 11:27–29.)

3. How are prophetic warnings different from prophetic judgments? Why is it incorrect to call warnings judgments?

4. In regard to judgment, what does it mean to say that there are things that Jesus did, is doing and will do that we simply will never do?

5. In what way do we put a stumbling block in front of pre-Christians when we attribute every natural disaster to God? What paradigm does the Bible give us to present instead? (See *School of the Prophets* pages 127–128.)

_____

_____

_____

DAY 5

JUDGMENT OR CONSEQUENCES?

Above all, keep fervent in your love for one another, because love covers a multitude of sins.

1 Peter 4:8

Sometimes I find it hard to convince prophetic people that there is a difference between judgment and suffering the natural consequences of our actions. Often, prophetic people get judgment and punishment mixed up with sowing and reaping, but these things are not at all the same.

Read the example of little Johnny in today's book pages and the difference I am talking about will become clearer to you. Judgment requires a decree of punishment from the Judge, whereas sowing simply results in reaping the consequences (good or bad) of your actions.

It bothers me when prophets and prophetesses take the responsibility and authority incumbent in their office and use it to pronounce judgment against those suffering the natural results of their actions. They gleefully (or so it seems to me) point to the negative consequences falling upon someone's life and declare that the sinner is under the judgment of God. That is a far cry from carrying out the ministry of reconciliation we have been given this side of the cross.

Certainly, those who hold a prophetic office are responsible to direct, correct and warn those under their authority. But they are also responsible to establish their prophetic ministry based on love, not judgment. Love can make all the difference to someone, as it has to me on more than one occasion.

- Today's Scripture reading: Galatians 6:6–10; 2 Corinthians 5:14–21
- Today's reading from *School of the Prophets*: pages 128–130

Questions to Consider ————————————————————————

1. Have you met leaders in the Church who are continually focused on identifying the judgments of God supposedly coming upon other people's lives? (Or have you been such a leader yourself?) In what ways does this go against the role of the prophet or prophetess in these New Testament/New Covenant days?

—————————————————————————————————————

—————————————————————————————————————

—————————————————————————————————————

2. What do you think I mean by my statement in the book that sowing and reaping is not judgment? How would you explain the difference in your own words? (See *School of the Prophets* page 128.)

—————————————————————————————————————

—————————————————————————————————————

—————————————————————————————————————

3. Besides the little Johnny example that I gave in the book, can you think of another example of sowing and reaping that has nothing to do with the judgment of God? Why do you think so many prophetic people are quick to call such natural consequences judgments?

—————————————————————————————————————

—————————————————————————————————————

—————————————————————————————————————

4. I told you in today's reading about the great prophet Bob Jones, who filled my life with love. Have you had someone in your life who was always quick to speak mercy, grace, life and peace to you? How did that person's love make a difference? Can you be that kind of person in someone else's life?

—————————————————————————————————————

—————————————————————————————————————

—————————————————————————————————————

■ Session 5 Life Application

Think about the chart we looked at in this session that summarizes the gift of prophecy versus the office of prophet/prophetess. I realize that not everyone reading these pages and doing this study will be counted among those holding the office of a prophet or prophetess (though many will). But all believers should be counted among those on the other side—those who operate in the gift of prophecy. That is, after all, what Paul expected when he instructed us all to desire earnestly the spiritual gifts, *especially* prophecy (see 1 Corinthians 14:1–5).

If you have never moved in the realm of the prophetic, take a few minutes right now to identify why not. Was it a lack of knowledge about the gift's availability to every believer? Remember, at Bethel we train everyone in this area of hearing from God, even the elderly and little children. You can learn to operate in this gift, too.

Was it fear of making a mistake or getting a word wrong? Remember that perfect love casts out fear; God loves you and wants you to operate in the gifts of the Spirit. We will address fear further in one of the sessions ahead, when we talk about equipping people in the prophetic ministry.

Was it not being in an atmosphere in which the gift could flow or not having an opportunity in which to try it? If you are part of a *School of the Prophets* group study, your group is an ideal place in which to get some practice. You can talk to your group leader more about that.

■ Session 5 Video Guide

1. You can't _____ the _____ of prophecy.

2. The gift of prophecy is a gift of the _____ _____; the office of the prophet is a gift of _____.

3. No matter how many gifts the Holy Spirit has to give, we are taught to _____ _____ the gift of _____.

4. The gift of prophecy _____ up, _____ up and _____ people near.

5. The fruits of the Spirit are a sign that you are _____ in God; the gifts of the Spirit are a sign that you've received an _____ from God, which is a free _____.

6. God has called both _____ to the _____ of prophet or prophetess.

7. If I am a prophet or prophetess, the gift is not _____ I _____, it's _____ I _____.

8. The _____ of the office of a prophet is _____ the _____.

9. A prophet must be _____ by God AND have _____ to lead.

10. Often God calls us, and _____ people _____ the call.

11. We _____ prophets; we don't _____ them.

12. There's a huge difference between a _____ and a _____.

13. Don't do with _____ what you should do with _____ (fatherhood and motherhood).

The Role
of the Prophet

Prophets give people eyes to see and ears to hear. One of the most important functions prophets and prophetesses have in the Body of Christ is to equip each member of the Church to hear from God for himself or herself, and for others in need. It is one sign of a highly dysfunctional spiritual community when the prophets or prophetesses become the main source of hearing from God. The primary responsibility of the office of the prophet and prophetess is to create a prophetic community where every member of the Body understands how to give and receive prophetic words.

School of the Prophets, pages 142–143

— DAY 1 —
"CAN THESE BONES LIVE?"

Death and life are in the power of the tongue.

Proverbs 18:21

Today, God is asking us as prophets and prophetesses the same question He asked Ezekiel in the valley of dry bones: "Can these bones live?" (Ezekiel 37:3). You remember what happened in that valley, right? A mighty army emerged as Ezekiel prophesied life into those bones with his words. As I say in today's reading, that was a foretaste of the prophetic office's most important role in our times—breathing life into an army of believers who will rise up and once again turn the world upside down.

In this session of our study, we will talk about a number of prophetic roles. We will talk about how prophets and prophetesses are builders with their words and equippers of the saints. We will talk about how they commission leaders, act as God's Secret Service and protect nations. Each of these roles is important, but speaking life rather than death is absolutely crucial. Building up the Body with our words is a vital element in the success of any project. Haggai and Zechariah are our examples of that in the book of Ezra. I talk more about that in today's reading. I also talk about four points for you to keep in mind that will strengthen your prophetic ministry and help you become a successful builder.

Over and over again throughout history, the devil has underestimated the life and power that can come out of death and dead bones. As God's prophets and prophetesses, we know better. Think about the cross, where Satan made his biggest mistake in underestimating a weakened Christ, a tattered band of followers and a few sorrowful women. I am sure you remember what happened in that dark valley, too. The Light of the world rose out of the tomb, an event that the prophets of God had predicted thousands of years ahead of time! The devil just was not listening closely enough when the prophets of God were "seeing" a deadly situation through the eyes of God and calling forth life from it.

- Today's Scripture reading: Ezekiel 37:1–10; Luke 4:1–13
- Today's reading from *School of the Prophets*: pages 131–137

Questions to Consider

1. What is the choice before the prophets and prophetesses of our day as they stand in the valley of decision? (See *School of the Prophets* page 132.) Why can it be said that the future of our nations hangs in the balance as the world waits for a decision?

2. Like William Wallace in the film *Braveheart*, how is it the responsibility of prophets and prophetesses to rise up and "pick a fight" against overwhelming odds in crucial moments? (See *School of the Prophets* page 134.)

3. What does it mean to say that prophets and prophetesses release declarations of hope in the midst of a house of horrors? What result does that have on the demonic realm? (See *School of the Prophets* page 134.)

4. According to Ezra, many people played a part in the rebuilding of the Temple—the people who were the laborers, the project managers who oversaw the work, the kings who supported it with their decrees and finances and even spiritual advisors. But when push came to shove, who really made the project work, and why? (See *School of the Prophets* page 137.)

— DAY 2 —

THE HEART OF PROPHECY

One who speaks in a tongue edifies himself, but one who prophesies edifies the church.

1 Corinthians 14:4

The heart of prophecy is to edify the Church. Those of us called to the office of prophet or prophetess edify the Church by faithfully fulfilling the roles God has assigned us. Today's reading in *School of the Prophets* focuses on two of our roles: prophets as builders and prophets as equippers.

Prophesying and building are practically synonymous. We saw in Day 1 of this session how the people were successful in rebuilding the Temple *through* the prophesying of Haggai and Zechariah. The Greek word for *edify* in the passage above literally means "to build a house," and that is what we prophets do with our words. We speak into people's hearts, and our words become living stones in them that they can build upon. It is an amazing process, and the more we build in people's hearts and lives, the brighter their light becomes in the darkest places on the planet. In a sense, we are prophesying over the world's destruction sites and seeing them transformed into construction sites for the Kingdom.

Of course building projects require laborers, which brings us to our prophetic role as equippers of the saints. Along with the other fivefold ministers, we equip the saints with the tools they need to carry out the Kingdom's extensive building plans all over the earth. Specifically, we prophets and prophetesses help people become discerning and solid in their doctrine, and we help them speak the truth in love and grow in the gift of prophecy available to every believer.

I talk more about all these things in today's book reading, but what it boils down to is that prophets give people eyes to see and ears to hear from God for themselves and for others in need. And that builds the Church in strength and power to carry out God's call.

- Today's Scripture reading: Romans 12
- Today's reading from *School of the Prophets*: pages 137–144

Questions to Consider _____

1. Because the call to the office comes from God, prophets do not reproduce other prophets. They should, however, be imparting and growing what in others? (See *School of the Prophets* page 140.)

_____

_____

_____

2. I used the unusual metaphor in today's reading of the fivefold ministry being like a soda fountain. What does the size of the container you bring to the fountain represent in your life? How is the size of the container you are bringing to the prophetic "dispenser" increasing as you move through this study?

_____

_____

_____

3. What do you think it means to say that the value you place on an office in the Church determines the power you receive from it? (See *School of the Prophets* page 142.)

_____

_____

_____

4. What does it signify about a spiritual community when its prophets and prophetesses become everyone's main source of hearing from God? (See *School of the Prophets* page 143.) What might be some of the results of that scenario?

_____

_____

_____

5. How does the presence of "prophetic superstars" sometimes leave other people feeling unequipped and disqualified? Have you ever experienced that? What do you think can be done to change that dynamic?

_____

_____

_____

— DAY 3 —

COMMISSIONING LEADERS

Do not neglect the spiritual gift within you, which was bestowed
on you through prophetic utterance with the laying on of hands.

1 Timothy 4:14

As a prophet, I have often had the privilege of commissioning leaders into their divine call. Many times the commissioning has taken place inside the Church; many times it has taken place in the secular realm of government in various countries. Commissioning leaders is one of the most exciting things I do in carrying out my office.

We frequently see prophets commissioning leaders in the Old Testament; I give you some of my favorite examples of that in today's reading. We also see it in the New Testament, for example when the presbytery commissioned Timothy. I am not sure we see the prophetic commissioning of leaders taking place as much today as it did in Scripture, although I think we should see more of it.

Prophetic commissioning imparts something vital to those on the receiving end. Moses passed on his mantle of leadership and his authority to Joshua, and Paul desired to see the believers at Rome so that he could impart a spiritual gift to them. Without commissioning, something will be missing that a leader needs in order to function well in his or her position. Every position of authority comes from God (see Romans 13:1), and every mission from God comes with a mantle that gives the person who steps into that mission the supernatural ability to complete it. The mantle stays with the mission, which I talk about more in today's reading.

Commissioning someone involves more than a ceremony; it is the *Yes* and *Amen* of God establishing a person in his or her divine mission. I often wonder how many leaders are not carrying the mantle or anointing they need in their office because they were not prophetically commissioned, and how many offices have the wrong leader in place. The prophets and prophetesses of today need to take on their God-given role of commissioning leaders, so that we can all go on to fulfill the Great Commission.

- Today's Scripture reading: Romans 13:1–7; Exodus 17:8–13
- Today's reading from *School of the Prophets*: pages 144–150

Questions to Consider

1. Think about someone you know on whom a mantle of anointing obviously rests. Do you know the specifics of how the person was commissioned to wear the mantle? What effect does that mantle have on the person's leadership abilities and presence?

2. Why does a mantle stay with a mission rather than remaining on a particular person? (See *School of the Prophets* page 147.)

3. What was the significance of Eleazar the priest bringing only the Urim and not the Thummim to Joshua's commissioning? What does this suggest about how the prophetic ministry functions at times? (See *School of the Prophets* pages 146–147.)

— DAY 4 —

GOD'S SECRET SERVICE

Surely the Lord GOD does nothing unless He reveals His secret counsel to His servants the prophets.

Amos 3:7

If God had a Secret Service working for Him here on earth, it would be made up of His prophets and prophetesses. He trusts us with highly classified information, as Amos 3:7 reveals, sometimes sharing things that He wants us to address only in prayer. When you are called to a prophetic office, you are also automatically employed by God's Secret Service.

The Prophetic Secret Service is all about protection, too, just like the U.S. Secret Service—except we are both the protected and the protectors. God protects those He calls into prophetic office, sometimes long before they take up the prophetic mantle. I tell the story in today's reading of one time that God supernaturally protected me before I was even a believer (and it was not the only time). Throughout my life, I have known the favor and protection of God. I am grateful that He protects the people He promotes.

We prophets and prophetesses are also protectors of others, as well as of the nations. No one who is aware of what is going on in the world can doubt that there are nations and people groups on this planet that are bent on the destruction of others. Prophets and prophetesses are often called on to prophesy against violent acts of terror and intercede on behalf of the nations. It happened countless times in the Old Testament, and I can attest from personal experience that it still happens today.

- Today's Scripture reading: 2 Kings 6; Psalm 34
- Today's reading from *School of the Prophets*: pages 150–155

Questions to Consider _____

1. How does it stand to reason that we prophets and prophetesses should ask God for permission to share the things He reveals to us? (See *School of the Prophets* pages 150–151.)

_____

_____

_____

2. Does the fact that God sometimes protects His prophets even when they are wrong mean He condones their bad behavior? What does it mean, if not that?

_____

_____

_____

3. Tell briefly about an experience you may have had similar to mine where God's supernatural protection over you spared your life or saved you from injury.

_____

_____

_____

4. Why is it important to realize that this side of the cross, the prophetic role of protecting nations does not have to do with judgment or a "good guy, bad guy" mentality? (See *School of the Prophets* page 154.)

_____

_____

_____

—— DAY 5 ——

THE HERE AND NOW

And He will judge between the nations, and will render decisions for many peoples; and they will hammer their swords into plowshares and their spears into pruning hooks. Nation will not lift up sword against nation, and never again will they learn war.

Isaiah 2:4

Why not here, and why not now? That is the final question I ask in this session's final reading from *School of the Prophets*. In the here and now, why not look for increase instead of decrease, growth instead of decline, peace instead of war, and the rise of the Kingdom, not the deepening of darkness over our nations?

In today's book reading, I quote a prophecy I gave a few years back over my country, America, in the midst of widespread economic and political turmoil. The word that came forth was far more positive than negative—quite the reverse of much that comes out of the "Prophets of Doom" in our day. And much of that word has come to pass already, some of it immediately after the prophecy, as you will read about in *School of the Prophets*.

I believe there will always be trouble in or between nations, until the King comes again. Yet I also believe that we are entering a time when we will find a way this side of the cross to love our enemies, reconcile people to God and hold on to our Kingdom core values, all while protecting our nations through our supernatural gifts. Good things are on the horizon for my country and for other nations. Some good things will come out of the governmental arena in various places, and some good things will come from the people themselves (particularly in my country). But good things are on the way. That is my deep-down prophetic sense. Why not live with that expectation? Why not look for the spread of the Kingdom in the here and now?

- Today's Scripture reading: Isaiah 9:1–7
- Today's reading from *School of the Prophets*: pages 156–160

Questions to Consider _____

1. What was your response to reading my prophecy of February 19, 2012? Did it give you hope for America and other countries like China, especially in hindsight now that some of it has already come to pass?

_____

_____

_____

2. People often look to the political realm to usher in positive change, especially here in America, but does it always have to come from the people we vote for in our elections? Where else can dramatic change for the better arise? (See *School of the Prophets* pages 157–158.)

_____

_____

_____

3. Take a little time to pray into Isaiah 2:2–4, as I have been doing. What are a couple possible supernatural ramifications of that 2,500-year-old prophecy that you see for the here and now as you pray and meditate on that passage?

_____

_____

_____

Session 6 Life Application

In this session, we covered a number of roles that the prophets and prophetesses of our time are responsible to carry out. Look at the following list of the roles we discussed and choose the one that you learned the most about by going through this session:

• Building with words
• Equipping the saints
• Commissioning leaders
• Keeping God's secrets
• Protecting the nations

If you hold the office of a prophet or prophetess, ask the Holy Spirit what you need to do to function more effectively in the role you learned the most about (as well as the other roles). Talk to another trustworthy believer in your prophetic community and get some input about how you might carry out that role in practical ways. Evaluate how your prophetic ministry might change and become more effective as you carry out that role, and then ask God to give you opportunities to put what you have learned into practice.

1. Words become _____. We're not on the eve of _____; we're on the eve of _____.

2. _____ change history. Sometimes they change history on their _____ in prophetic prayer, and sometimes they change history when they prophesy the _____ to kings.

3. Romans 12:6 says, "Since we have gifts that differ according to the _____ given to us, each of us is to _____ them accordingly: if prophecy, according to the proportion of his _____ . . ."

4. Grace is the _____ _____ of God that gives me the ability to do what I couldn't do one _____ before I received the grace.

5. The _____ job of the _____ is to equip the saints with pastoral grace so that the _____ can take care of the saints.

6. The goal of the _____ is that you would have eyes to see and ears to hear so that the _____ can take care of the _____ that the Body has for prophetic revelation and prophetic ministry to comfort, build up and console.

7. Prophets _____ leaders.

8. Oftentimes God calls _____ to _____ kings and governors and mayors.

9. If we (as prophets) _____ from people who don't know God, there will be no _____ in their life.

10. We create _____ of prophetic _____ where people can have experiences with God and become who they were meant to be.

BUILDING
A PROPHETIC
COMMUNITY

In so many churches I visit, there is no prophetic culture because there are no coaches and no referees. It is just your basic prophetic pickup game. If prophets and prophetesses are going to transform dysfunctional prophetic ministries into healthy prophetic communities, we must create the expectation among our prophetic people that they are playing on a team. There is no place for selfish, independent and/or rebellious people who do not know how to honor leadership. The greatest challenge that many of us will experience is shifting the mindset of our prophetic people from being on the playground to being on global strike teams.

School of the Prophets, page 170

— DAY 1 —

RISKY BUSINESS

Without faith it is impossible to please Him, for he who comes to God must believe that He is and that He is a rewarder of those who seek Him.

Hebrews 11:6

Christians often talk about fulfilling their divine call in the sense of it being an adventure and a challenge and a joy and many other things, but one description you do not hear for it very often is that it is risky business. Yet I think Scripture clearly shows that risk is actually a part of the nature of God. He took a huge risk in giving us a free will and all kinds of options to choose from, right from the start in the Garden. If we are like Him, risk-taking for the Kingdom will become part of our nature, too.

To develop a healthy prophetic culture, which is what this session focuses on, we need to cultivate an element of risk in the people we are growing. Operating in the gifts and calling of God does not come without risk—unless we remove the risk artificially. Religion tries to sanitize people by eliminating their choices, which supposedly removes the risk of making bad choices. I see that not as sanctification, but as control. That kind of control can result in false behavior patterns that fall by the wayside pretty quickly when believers make their way out from behind the four walls of a controlling church into the world's "jungle."

When it comes to training and equipping prophetic people, we cannot afford to remove the risks. Learning to operate in the prophetic is simply a risky business. We need to face the fact that it is impossible to train our prophetic people in the zoo and have them ready to face the reality of the jungle! (I will explain more about that statement in today's book reading.) I realize that risk taking ourselves and letting those under our authority take risks can result in some messes to clean up and some exposed flaws to deal with. But spiritual maturity is another result born out of that process. And that is worth the risk!

- Today's Scripture reading: Galatians 5:13–25
- Today's reading from *School of the Prophets*: pages 161–169

Questions to Consider _____

    1. What is the major difference between prophetic ministry and a healthy prophetic culture? (See *School of the Prophets* pages 162–163.) Why do healthy cultures need proactive leaders rather than inactive or reactive ones?

    2. Why do you think God wants to give people choices? What is His reaction when we make wrong choices?

    3. In what way can prophetic ministry grow best in an R&D (research and development) culture? Why does a "zero defect" core value shut down that growth? (See *School of the Prophets* pages 166–167.)

    4. What does it mean to say that many spiritual leaders create cultures that refuse to tolerate sin because they feel powerless to help people process their way to purity? What is the value in processing through to purity rather than removing all risk of sin?

— Day 2 —

Coaching Team Players

God is not a God of confusion but of peace. . . . All things must be done properly and in an orderly manner.

1 Corinthians 14:33, 40

Have you ever had a coach who had a huge positive impact on your life? So many coaches make an amazing difference not just in a young person's skill level in a particular sport, but in his or her success level in life. Becoming a team player with a good coach can go a long way toward growing young people in both maturity and character.

The same exact thing applies in the lives of our prophetic people. In developing a healthy prophetic community, we have to get our people to understand that they are team players. And those of us involved in leading a prophetic community have to coach our people well. When we can help them become dedicated team players and coach them well, it goes a long way toward growing them in both maturity and character.

What does good coaching in the prophetic realm involve? We will look at that closely today and in the remaining days of this session. As prophetic coaches, we empower our people to experiment with their skills, and even to make some mistakes and clean up the resulting messes. We allow them to practice their skills and gain some experience so that when it is time to go out into the jungle, as we talked about in Day 1, they are ready to form a prophetic strike team and get into the game, pressing on to victory.

Besides coaching our people, though, sometimes we also have to act as referees. That means bringing some rules of order into the game and confronting players who are behaving in a way that hurts the team's efforts. I talk a lot in today's reading about how we can skillfully confront the prophetic people whom we have empowered to minister on our team. This is an important area for leaders to become equipped in because the need for honorable confrontation in a prophetic community will arise—you can count on it. I hope today's lesson will go a long way toward equipping you in this area.

Many churches lack a well-developed prophetic culture because they lack prophetic coaches and referees. Their people are just playing your basic prophetic pickup game, which can be exciting in the moment. They could go a lot further and have more of an impact for the Kingdom, though, if they were team players with committed, encouraging coaches and referees. Let's do all we can to provide those under our authority in our prophetic communities with the best coaching possible.

- Today's Scripture reading: Ephesians 4:14–32
- Today's reading from *School of the Prophets*: pages 169–176

Questions to Consider _____

1. What coaching did Paul give to those in the Corinthian church who were turning prophetic ministry into a free-for-all? (See *School of the Prophets* page 170.)

_____

_____

_____

2. What was one of David's biggest flaws in his leadership ability? What kind of issues did it cause for him and for those under his authority? (See *School of the Prophets* page 171.) What do we need to do to avoid that flaw in ourselves?

_____

_____

_____

3. What do you think it means to say that prophetic revelation is never discovered behind the iron bars of the zoo?

_____

_____

_____

4. Confrontation should never include anger, punishment or a desire to prove yourself right. From today's lesson, name two or three things it should include that most stood out to you.

_____

_____

_____

— DAY 3 —

SUPERNATURAL INOCULATIONS

> You should diligently keep the commandments of the LORD your
> God, and His testimonies.
>
> Deuteronomy 6:17

Testimonies are a powerful catalyst to a healthy prophetic culture. Why? Because they act as supernatural inoculations against fear and negativity. Prophetic people are frequently hypersensitive to any negative spiritual activity going on in or around them, which can cause them to become problem focused, anxious and even fearful. That drains their anointing for ministry. Recounting testimonies of God's goodness and power, however, drains the infection of fear.

Proverbs 17:22 (NIV) tells us, "A cheerful heart is good medicine." There is no better medicine than recounting the things God has already done in our lives. Hearing testimonies cheers us up and gives us hope, no matter what challenges we are facing. Because testimonies remind us of what God has already accomplished for us, they raise our expectations about what He will yet do. They get us excited about the future as we remember the past.

As I tell you in today's book reading, we at Bethel Church steward the testimonies the same way that some people steward property or finances. Testimonies are precious to us. You might say we have a whole medicine cabinet full of them, and we keep it very well stocked.

What about you? Do you need to start stocking up on some powerful spiritual medicine and start giving your prophetic people supernatural inoculations? Then encourage testimonies. (We will talk a little more about how to do that in Day 4 just ahead.) Testimonies will fight the infection of fear and bring your prophetic community new health and strength.

- Today's Scripture reading: Deuteronomy 6:10–19; 1 John 4:15–19
- Today's reading from *School of the Prophets*: pages 176–179

Questions to Consider _____

1. Why do you think it is so easy for prophetic people to fall into the trap of becoming hypersensitive to negative spiritual activity? How are testimonies one cure for that?

_____

_____

_____

2. What is fear actually faith in? What belief lies at the root of fear? (See *School of the Prophets* page 177.) How do testimonies lay the ax to that root?

_____

_____

_____

3. What does it mean to say that thanksgiving gestates in the garden of recollection and reflection on the acts of God? How do testimonies grow thanksgiving in our hearts?

_____

_____

_____

4. What did the sons of Ephraim forget, which in King David's estimation caused them to turn back in the day of battle and fail to accomplish their mission? (See *School of the Prophets* page 178.)

_____

_____

_____

5. How can testimonies help you come to the table with supernatural solutions already in mind before you even "get down to business" and approach your life and ministry's practical problems?

_____

_____

_____

— Day 4 —

Shepherding Superheroes

Let no one keep defrauding you of your prize by delighting in self-abasement and the worship of angels, taking his stand on visions he has seen, inflated without cause by his fleshly mind.

Colossians 2:18

As we finish this session, in today's lesson and in Day 5 I want to focus on a few practical tips that will help you shift the atmosphere of your prophetic community into a faith culture. If you will put these tips into practice, the faith and strength of those you are responsible to shepherd will grow.

We talked already about one of these tips, encouraging testimonies. Let me add to what I said in Day 3 that the way to encourage testimonies is first to begin every meeting by having people share with the group their prophetic exploits. Do not skip this vital exercise if you are looking to build a faith culture. Make time for it, and make a point of stressing its importance.

Second, make sure you wisely guide these times of testimony. You will probably need to do some coaching about who shares what and when, which brings us to my other tip for today, shepherding the superheroes among your prophetic people. There are those who are spiritual superheroes, and then there are those with the superhero syndrome. There are also those somewhere in between, who are capable of growing from the syndrome into the reality. They all need coaches who will make sure everybody gets into the game, and perhaps even more, they need referees who will make sure everybody plays by the rules and benefits the team with their behavior.

Those who are beginners among you may need extra encouragement to become comfortable sharing in front of the rest, and those who are hyper-spiritual may need some firm guidance and loving confrontation so that what they share is appropriate, not arising from their personal issues instead of heavenly inspiration. Today's reading in the book goes into more detail about how to handle these different personalities as you work toward building a faith culture.

- Today's Scripture reading: Colossians 2
- Today's reading from *School of the Prophets*: pages 179–182

Questions to Consider _____

1. What does it accomplish to have your people begin every meeting by sharing their testimonies, particularly stories about their prophetic exploits? If your prophetic culture does not already include this faith builder, what steps will you take to begin putting it into practice?

2. How do prophetic superheroes raise the bar in a prophetic community? How do they sometimes intimidate beginners who may have less anointing? In what way can we as leaders help balance these two effects? (See *School of the Prophets* pages 180–181.)

3. What is the difference between moving in high levels of spiritual anointing (actually being a prophetic superhero) and being hyper-spiritual (having the superhero syndrome)?

4. Name a few ways in which leaders of prophetic communities can help hyper-spiritual people develop and grow in character.

— Day 5 —

Unshackled and Uninhibited

For God has not given us a spirit of fear, but of power and of love
and of a sound mind.

2 Timothy 1:7 NKJV

Today we will look at two more tips I have for you that will help you build a faith culture in your prophetic community. The first is that you need to identify the superheroes in disguise among you, and the second is that you need to help the fearful get free. When you get these two groups of people, the disguised superheroes and those in bondage to fear, to come out of hiding and step into all God has planned for them, it will revolutionize their ministry and that of the prophetic community you oversee.

In Day 4 we talked about the different kinds of spiritual superheroes among us—genuine superheroes, those with the superhero syndrome, and those somewhere in between, who are in the process of moving into maturity. There is another kind, however—the superheroes in disguise. These people are also genuine superheroes, but they are hidden behind unique personalities that might not make you look at them twice as superhero material. They may not be the most charismatic go-getters in your crowd, but God has chosen to use them in extraordinary ways. Identifying superheroes in disguise in the community I oversee has taught me more than once that God's choices may differ radically from what I expect. He can choose and use anyone He pleases, even if His choices surprise me. (Think of how surprised the apostles were when God extended salvation to the Gentiles and baptized them in the Holy Spirit.) I do my best to bring the people He chooses out of hiding and grow them in their gift.

The other prophetic people I make an effort to identify and bring out of hiding are those bound by fear. I know it can be easier all around to let them retreat into a corner on the fringe of your group, where they watch what goes on but never really participate. That is not good for them or for your group. With patience and determination, I seek out the fearful and introduce them to their biggest fears so that they can overcome them, which is absolutely crucial if they are ever going to accomplish all God intends in their lives and as part of a prophetic community. Eventually they thank me for it! The fearful in your group will thank you, too, when you help them realize what it is like to walk unshackled and uninhibited, free to become the mighty sons and daughters of the living God who bring His light and life into dark places.

- Today's Scripture reading: Acts 10:34–48
- Today's reading from *School of the Prophets*: pages 182–186

Questions to Consider

1. If you have ever looked at someone and thought, *I can't believe God chose him (or her) to do that*, you know what I mean when I say that sometimes God's choices of the people He uses can surprise me. What about you? Is there anything surprising about God choosing you for the role you play in His Kingdom?

2. On one level it seems a little unkind and unfeeling to discern what people are afraid of and then purposely guide that giant into their land and introduce them to it, but what good effects can that painful moment have on them and their ministry long-term?

3. Fear can be contagious, but so can freedom. I give you an example in today's book reading of how freedom spread through an entire class at our supernatural school when one young lady was forced to face her fears. Describe a time when you saw freedom and/or courage spread through a group of people because one person took action first and faced an issue or a fear head-on.

Go back for a few moments and reread the short section in *School of the Prophets* where I talk about how prophetic revelation grows best in an R&D culture (pages 166–168). Evaluate how well the prophetic community you are involved with makes room for R&D in prophetic ministry. Is there room at all to experiment, make messes, learn from a few failures and clean things up afterward? Or have people tried to apply the "zero defects" core value to the prophetic ministry, causing stunted growth as a result? List two or three ways you might start encouraging more of an R&D culture within your prophetic community (without compromising in areas like character that ought to have zero defects).

Now take this application to a personal level. In your personal ministry, list two or three ways you might start stepping out and taking some risks to grow prophetically, without compromising your character. Run your ideas past another prophetic believer whom you work closely with in your group, and ask him or her to come alongside you in your efforts. If you are not the leader of your prophetic community, you might also talk to the leader who oversees you about what you are learning in this study and how you desire to apply it in practical ways. Ask your leader for insights and suggestions related to carrying out this life application.

■ **Session 7 Video Guide** —————————————————————————

1. There's a difference between prophetic _____ and a prophetic
   _____ .

2. There are _____ and _____, _____ and _____,
   metaphorically speaking, who help us learn the "game" of prophecy.

3. It's not practice that makes perfect, it's _____ _____ that
   makes perfect. If you practice something the _____ way long
   enough, it becomes a _____ and it's difficult to change.

4. It's okay for leadership to _____ how we're doing (in prophetic
   ministry). _____ is the way we grow.

5. Part of growing a prophetic community is that to the level that you
   _____ people, you _____ them.

6. We don't want to develop a culture of _____, because as soon
   as we do that, we take away the culture where we're confronting in a
   _____ way.

7. We have to _____ and _____ with _____ in mind.

8. You may be determining your _____, your sphere of influence,
   by your _____ .

9. It doesn't hurt to keep _____; it's not the fear of man. You give
   _____ to whom _____ is due.

10. God likes _____. Paul said let _____ _____ be done
    decently and in order.

11. As prophets and prophetesses, it's our job to help _____ and
    ref our people so that we actually begin to help create a prophetic
    _____ and a prophetic _____ .

12. A prophetic culture is a culture of _____, but it's also a culture
    of _____ .

STANDING BEFORE KINGS; NOBLE PROPHETS

God is calling us as noble prophets and prophetesses, who are comfortable in the courts of kings (and who also love the poor and broken), to understand the epoch season in which we live, so that we can rise up and positively influence the course of history. He has empowered us to cast off the shackles of judgment and begin to prophesy constructively to the hurting, wounded and depressed. God has also commissioned us as His New Testament prophets and prophetesses to train and equip the King's royal army of saints so that they can displace darkness and build with light.

Some of us may never grace the threshold of a palace or dine with a world leader, yet we are still called to speak for the King so that we can bring hope to the hopeless and courage to the fainthearted. It is in the darkest situations that we must call for light, it is in the dirtiest souls that we must look for treasure and it is in the toughest of times that we must strengthen the weary.

School of the Prophets, pages 229–230

— Day 1 —

Transforming the Nations

Then Jesus came to them and said, "All authority in heaven and on earth has been given to me. Therefore go and make disciples of all nations, baptizing them in the name of the Father and of the Son and of the Holy Spirit, and teaching them to obey everything I have commanded you. And surely I am with you always, to the very end of the age."

Matthew 28:18–20

Prophets and prophetesses are called to become cultural catalysts that transform the nations . . . but how? A lot of nations, and a lot of individuals on a personal level, have no interest whatsoever in being transformed. But Jesus commanded us first to make disciples and then to teach them, so it can be done. It is a matter of motivating people and nations to want to learn.

Then the question becomes, what would get them motivated? An encounter with God Himself, through their exposure to us, would do it. If you know Him, you already know He is irresistible. Others will think so, too, once they start getting to know Him through you and me.

It is what happened in the story of Joseph, which we will look at in-depth in today's reading from *School of the Prophets*, a reading that is longer than usual because we have so much to gain from looking at the ways and means Joseph had of becoming a cultural catalyst. His influence on the Egyptian culture, which he entered as a slave and exited as one of the most powerful rulers the country had ever known, was boundless.

Joseph started out with a spiritual heritage, walked in the favor of God, became a father of his adoptive nation, and with his own father, Jacob, loved and blessed that nation, resulting in some stunning transformation. I have learned from Joseph's story every step of the way as I have pondered over the years how to become more of a cultural catalyst to transform the nations. Along with the prophet Daniel, whose story we will look at in Day 2, Joseph has had a huge impact on the way I approach prophetic ministry.

I believe these two inspiring stories of Joseph and Daniel will have a profound impact on your prophetic ministry as well. Learning more about these two prophets will give you a desire to bless the world and its peoples as they did, and as prophets and prophetesses should.

- Today's Scripture reading: 2 Timothy 3; Romans 4
- Today's reading from *School of the Prophets*: pages 187–203

Questions to Consider —————————————

1. As Bill Johnson says, the Church needs to learn to answer the questions the world is not asking, but should be. What does that mean to you in the sense of creating learners and then teaching them?

   _____

   _____

   _____

2. Joseph and Daniel both guided Gentile kings into God's destiny for them and practically and supernaturally altered the history of godless and wicked nations for the better. From our look at Joseph so far, briefly identify a few things about his approach that made it possible for him to have such far-reaching impact.

   _____

   _____

   _____

3. While both are important ministries, what is the difference between being a prophet *to the nations* and being a prophet *of the nations*? (See *School of the Prophets* page 199.)

   _____

   _____

   _____

4. What is keeping the prophets of today from blessing the world the way Israel blessed Pharaoh? You might recognize that question as the one I posed at the end of today's book reading. Do you think anything should be keeping today's prophets from befriending and blessing the pharaohs of this present world? What might the impact of their prophetic blessing be?

   _____

   _____

   _____

— Day 2 —

Learning Their Language

Behold, I send you out as sheep in the midst of wolves; so be shrewd
as serpents and innocent as doves.

Matthew 10:16

Daniel was another prophet whose story has greatly impacted my own. He had a lot in common with Joseph, whom we discussed in Day 1. Their commonalities are character traits I have worked hard to pick up on in my ministry as a father of the nations. In particular, these two prophets had a huge capacity to forgive their enemies and even love them to the point that their enemies began to love them back. Both ended up serving, blessing and loving foreign kings. To do so, they learned the language and customs of the countries where they unwillingly wound up.

Both Joseph and Daniel laid down their own anger and agendas and worked to love the people whom they served. Remember that we talked back in Day 5 of Session 3 about how all our prophetic ministry should be rooted in love? The stories of Joseph and Daniel illustrate why. You can accomplish amazing things with love. I believe, in fact, that God gave these two men tremendous access to such powerful kings because they could love.

Can we, as prophets to and of the nations and as fathers and mothers of many nations, follow their example? Can we learn the language of cultures foreign to us and learn to love those whose core values differ so widely from our own? (This can be especially challenging if we are American; we tend to think our American core values are the same as the Kingdom's, which is not necessarily the case.)

It has been a balancing act for me to remain loyal and dedicated to my country first, but also to learn the language of my international "sons and daughters," who have an outlook so different from mine, and to love them. The Holy Spirit's direction is indispensable in maintaining a balance in this kind of prophetic ministry. Wherever we are called to minister, though, and whatever language they speak, one thing is sure—it is the language of love that is best understood.

- Today's Scripture reading: Daniel 4:1–27; Isaiah 45:1–7
- Today's reading from *School of the Prophets*: pages 203–211

Questions to Consider _____

1. What did Joseph and Daniel's great character, supernatural powers and extraordinary love make it possible for them to do for the Egyptians, Babylonians and Persians? (See *School of the Prophets* pages 207–208.)

   _____

   _____

   _____

2. Why is it beneficial to "learn the language" of a culture into which we are called to speak prophetically?

   _____

   _____

   _____

3. What does it mean to say that every country views world history through its own core perspectives? How does having an awareness of that fact increase our effectiveness in prophetic ministry?

   _____

   _____

   _____

4. Without the Holy Spirit's direction, how might our perspectives become tainted? How would this affect us as the spiritual fathers and mothers of other nations? (See *School of the Prophets* page 210.)

   _____

   _____

   _____

5. How can prophets and prophetesses be compared to yeast in the dough of society? How does God use us in that way? (See *School of the Prophets* page 210.)

_____

_____

_____

— Day 3 —
Honoring Prophetic Diversity

There are varieties of ministries, and the same Lord.

1 Corinthians 12:5

I see some of the DNA of Joseph and Daniel in myself and in our company of prophets at Bethel, and that is why we have taken such a close look at them in this session. While I have drawn much of my prophetic insight from their stories, however, I do realize that they are not the only model for prophetic ministry. They are one model out of many that Scripture shows us.

It takes all kinds of prophetic models to transform culture. In today's book reading, I list six different models for you. Perhaps you will relate more closely to one of them than to the model of ministry we see in Joseph and Daniel. Or maybe your prophetic DNA does not quite fit any of the models I list, which is fine. There are several more models in Scripture that I do not have room to cover in this study.

When it comes to the wide variety of prophetic models, it is important not to put God in a "prophetic box" by thinking that every other prophet and prophetess will carry out the call and ministry the same way we do. Honoring prophetic diversity is the high road we need to take as we work separately and together. Prophets and prophetesses who work from different models need to embrace each other in the unity of the Spirit, propelled by the bond of peace.

It has taken me a while to get on this high road, as I tell you in today's reading. God had to take me through the startling differences in the ministries of Jesus and John the Baptist and show me how they honored each other before I began to understand the importance of prophetic diversity. I hope today's lesson will bring that revelation to you more easily.

- Today's Scripture reading: Mark 1:4–8; John 2:1–11; 19:23
- Today's reading from *School of the Prophets*: pages 211–217

Questions to Consider _____

1. In what way do many prophetic people put God in a "prophetic box" and miss the greater revelation of His prophetic nature?

   _____

   _____

   _____

2. Before today's lesson, had you ever thought about the polar-opposite ways in which John the Baptist and Jesus approached ministry? What does their attitude toward each other teach us about finding unity in our prophetic diversity?

   _____

   _____

   _____

3. Does the idea that it takes all kinds of prophets and prophetesses to make the world go round also apply to other ministers and ministries? Briefly give an example, either from the prophetic or from a different area of ministry, where you have seen great power and effectiveness come out of the unity among those who have differing spiritual DNA.

   _____

   _____

   _____

—— DAY 4 ——
TIMING IS EVERYTHING

There is an appointed time for everything. And there is a time for every event under heaven. . . . He has made everything appropriate in its time.

Ecclesiastes 3:1, 11

God has called me into the realm of ministering to world leaders prophetically, and I believe He may also call you to that if you are reading these pages. The final chapter of *School of the Prophets*, which we will look at today and in Day 5 just ahead, deals specifically with the how-tos of ministering to high-level leaders. Whether the leaders you deal with are involved in the government, the Church or the corporate world, there are many things you can do (and not do) to increase your effectiveness in ministering to and blessing them.

If you are not called to this area of prophetic ministry, read on anyway. Whatever area God has called you to, you can be sure that He has equipped you with a special grace and supernatural faith to accomplish your mission, as He has done for me. It may be that in following through with the remainder of this study, you will find some tips and how-tos that you can practically apply in your area of influence as well.

Timing really is everything. I tell you in today's reading how one comment from Cindy Jacobs of Generals International unlocked for me a whole new world of ministering to political leaders. The key Cindy handed me had to do with timing. I had been anxious because I was not getting a word from God beforehand for political leaders with whom I was to meet, but Cindy told me that she gets words for them in the moment. That gave me the grace to walk into such meetings with complete peace, knowing that God would send what was needed at the exact time I needed it.

The other thing about timing in relation to governmental, Church or corporate leaders is that everyone wants their time. Time is these leaders' most valuable commodity, and they will not waste it on us twice if we do not value it. It is imperative that we stick to the schedule when meeting with high-level leadership. We need to honor the starting and ending time of our meeting, the amount of time leaders have set aside for us and any changes in schedule that they request (like extending our meeting because they want to hear more or needing to cut it short because they must deal with a crisis that arises).

Whether you tend to run early or late in your personal life, you need to make a firm commitment to run right on time in this kind of ministry to powerful leaders.

- Today's Scripture reading: Ecclesiastes 3:1–8
- Today's reading from *School of the Prophets*: pages 219–225

Questions to Consider _____

1. Did you notice that in my story of meeting with a world leader, he was told initially that I was a "futurist" rather than a prophet? How might that particular wording have opened the door for a meeting more quickly? How does this illustrate the importance of "learning the language" of those to whom we will minister?

_____

_____

_____

2. Since political leaders (and probably high-level leaders in many other arenas) are used to being diplomatic and gracious, can you think of some ways to avoid mistaking their kindness for receptivity? Why would that be important?

_____

_____

_____

3. Like most of us, you probably know from experience that nothing is more frustrating than having someone waste your time or throw you off schedule. We need to avoid doing that to high-level leaders at all costs, or our relationship with them will be short-lived and short-circuited. What are some ways you can think of in which you can allocate your meeting time with a high-level leader wisely?

_____

_____

_____

— DAY 5 —

SETTING THE GROUND RULES

The kingdom of the world has become the kingdom of our Lord
and of His Christ; and He will reign forever and ever.

Revelation 11:15

Whether we grace the threshold of palaces and dine with kings or work among the poor and broken, we are called to speak for the King and help usher in His Kingdom throughout the earth. He has called us to be fugitives from the law of averages, as I put it in today's book reading, and He has empowered us to step out as voices prophesying forth His word. Our mission, our mandate and our passion is to see the kingdom of this world become the Kingdom of our Lord, and to that end, we carry out our divine call as prophets and prophetesses.

In my years of traveling all over the world to minister prophetically to the political leaders of many nations, I have found that paying attention to certain key things maximizes my influence and effectiveness. In today's reading, I list these "lessons from the palace," which I have learned by experience. If you will set them as the ground rules of your ministry, I think you will find them equally as effective for you. (Again, although I am specifically addressing prophets and prophetesses called to the nations here, I think these ground rules can be beneficial for other kinds of ministry as well.)

Some of my ground rules are commonsense things we just need to be careful not to overlook in the busyness and uniqueness of what we are called to do. Some of them go deeper, involving a little analysis of the culture and people we are called to speak into. Some of them get personal, dealing with the appropriateness of our own mindset and behavior as we approach our meetings with high-level leaders. But at the heart, all of these ground rules are based on showing honor, respect and love to the ones to whom God sends us. Our character needs to reflect His character. More than anything else, it is His character—demonstrated through us as His love-filled ambassadors—that will draw the nations to our King.

- Today's Scripture reading: Colossians 4:2–6; Revelation 11:15–19
- Today's reading from *School of the Prophets*: pages 225–230

Questions to Consider

1. In ground rule 1, I talk about managing your appetites. Give a few examples of steps you can take to manage your appetites proactively.

2. In ground rule 2, I talk about confidentiality. Sometimes we think it is acceptable (I am not sure why) to share in a public testimony something exciting that happened in a private, personal meeting. In what way can this be damaging to a high-profile leader? What does it do to our own credibility?

3. In ground rule 3, I talk about requesting that your photograph be taken with famous people or leaders. Or more to the point, I talk about *not* requesting photographs. In this world of social networking on the Internet, why does it make sense not to put leaders on the spot by pressuring them to have their picture taken with you?

4. In ground rule 4, I talk about giving leaders your contact information rather than requesting theirs, and not giving their contact information out if you have it. Why is this an important way of developing and safeguarding your relationship with them?

5. In ground rule 5, I talk about bearing in mind that cell phones and the Internet are not secure communication devices, so it is necessary to watch what you say and how you say it. How might your awareness of this fact raise or lower a leader's trust in you?

_____

_____

_____

6. In ground rule 6, I talk about dressing appropriately for your meetings with leaders. Just a little carelessness in this area can result in giving major offense, whereas just a little research ahead of time can greatly increase a leader's receptivity to what you have to say. What are some ways in which you could determine appropriate attire for a meeting with a high-level leader?

_____

_____

_____

7. In ground rule 7, I talk about the vocabulary you use with a leader, in particular avoiding "Christianese" and clearly interpreting any metaphorical visions or dreams you have to relay. Pick two or three "Christianese" words you use frequently and redefine them here in everyday terms that would make them more accessible to an unbeliever.

_____

_____

_____

8. In ground rule 8, I talk about scrapping personal agendas as a means of avoiding getting into spiritual manipulation in your meetings. In that regard, what does it mean to say that we should not be doing with prophecy what we should be doing with discipleship?

_____

_____

_____

9. In ground rule 9, I reemphasize my point that it is important that we are culturalized into the countries in which we are called to disciple others (especially leaders). I also mention that it is wise to understand how different cultures view terms such as *Christian* before we start labeling ourselves or others. Briefly, what are some resources you can think of to use in preparing to minister to and disciple those of a different culture?

_____

_____

_____

■ Session 8 Life Application

Go back for a moment and review the list of six prophetic models I gave you in Day 3 of this session. (See *School of the Prophets* pages 212–214.) Notice that in relation to the government of their countries, some of the prophets and prophetesses were the leaders, some had a leadership gift and helped high-level leaders govern, some ministered prophetically to leaders on a personal level (but not governmental), some stood outside the palace and had an adversarial relationship with leaders, some dealt with the people of a country rather than its leaders and, finally, some ministered with an evangelistic mantle for the lost.

Prayerfully consider these models in relation to your prophetic ministry. (Or perhaps consider some models from Scripture that I have not listed here.) In what way do you personally relate to your country's governmental leaders or its people on a prophetic level? In other words, what kind of prophetic DNA do you have?

Next, consider what kind of relationship you have with prophets and prophetesses who have markedly different DNA than yours. After going through this session, do you see more clearly how your prophetic DNA may differ from other people's prophetic DNA, yet all of you can work in your own way toward the transformation of culture while honoring each other's efforts?

Ask the Holy Spirit to show you any areas where you may have fallen into a judgmental attitude about other prophetic ministries, as I did before God taught me the importance of prophetic diversity. Also pray about what steps you can take to correct your attitude and come into unity with other prophets and prophetesses who use a different model than yours to work toward the same goal as you—bringing the light of the Kingdom into every dark corner of the planet.

■ **Session 8 Video Guide**

1. A prophet to nations speaks *to* them about _____ they should do. A prophet of a nation becomes a _____ of that nation and a _____ *of* that nation.

2. You are inherently _____ because your daddy is _____.

3. Nobility in the _____ is that we get to bring out the _____ in people.

4. We need people who are full of _____, _____ and _____ to be interacting with and to be influencers of and leaders of nations.

5. God has a _____ for your life and _____ _____ to get you there.

6. Between the promise and the palace is a _____, and that process is what _____ your _____ so you can stay in the palace.

7. Small _____ open huge _____.

8. Daniel is part of the _____ without _____ his character.

9. It's hard for us to _____ from the outside what somebody's _____ is like on the inside.

10. The higher people get, the more _____ they are, and the more _____ they need.

11. It's Jesus who is _____ to people's souls, flowing _____ us—water to their souls and _____ on their destinies.

VIDEO GUIDE
ANSWER KEY

Session 1

1. shocked, Jesus
2. argue, Bible
3. life, best, ministry
4. receives, reward
5. anoint, sign, wonder
6. pathway, promise, palace

Session 2

1. root cause, lack, love
2. enemies, sons, unrighteous
3. hearts, don't
4. Old Covenant, hated, ushering
5. shift, world, deserve
6. works, His
7. judged, deal, Jesus
8. mercy, cross
9. reconcile, trespasses
10. ministry, enact judgment
11. tutor, Savior
12. role, role, judgment

Session 3

1. job, treasure
2. sin, flaws, goodness
3. dead body, step, choose
4. takes away, love, choice
5. last days, last day
6. judgment, never
7. last days, Spirit, flesh
8. great, glorious, saved
9. reconciliation, judgment
10. favorable, vengeance, thousands
11. Judgment Day, schizophrenic

Session 4

1. accent
2. view, you
3. lenses, see
4. angry, judgmental
5. affects, ministry
6. best, mercy, good
7. perfect, punishment, prophetic words
8. partnered, wrong
9. Word, Spirit, reality
10. encounter, encounter, love

Session 5

1. earn, gift
2. Holy Spirit, Christ
3. especially desire, prophecy
4. builds, cheers, calls
5. maturing, endowment, gift
6. genders, office
7. what, do, who, am
8. emphasis, equipping, saints
9. anointed, people
10. later, recognize
11. acknowledge, create
12. judgment, warning
13. prophecy, discipleship

Session 6

1. worlds, destruction, construction
2. Prophets, knees, direction
3. grace, exercise, faith
4. operational power, second
5. primary, pastor, saints
6. prophet, Body, need
7. commission
8. prophets, commission
9. withdraw, light
10. atmospheres, presence

Session 7 _____

1. ministry, community
2. fathers, mothers, coaches, referees
3. perfect practice, wrong, habit
4. critique, Feedback
5. empower, confront
6. punishment, redemptive
7. train, equip, deployment
8. metron, manifestation
9. protocol, honor, honor
10. order, all things
11. coach, community, culture
12. safety, risk

Session 8 _____

1. what, part, father
2. nobility, God
3. Kingdom, best
4. life, light, wisdom
5. purpose, 50 plans
6. process, refines, character
7. keys, doors
8. culture, compromising
9. judge, heart
10. isolated, encouragement
11. water, through, anointing

Kris Vallotton has been happily married to his wife, Kathy, since 1975. They have four children and eight grandchildren. Three of their children are in full-time vocational ministry. Kris is the co-founder and senior overseer of the Bethel School of Supernatural Ministry, which has grown to more than two thousand full-time students. He is also the founder and president of Moral Revolution, an organization dedicated to cultural transformation.

Kris is the senior associate leader of Bethel Church in Redding, California, and has served with Bill Johnson since 1978. He has written and co-authored numerous books, and his revelatory insight and humorous delivery make him a much-sought-after international conference speaker.

You can contact Kris or find out more about him and his other ministry materials at www.kvministries.com, or download the KV Ministries app on your smartphone. You can also follow Kris and Kathy on their Facebook fan page at www.facebook.com/kvministries.

NOTES

NOTES

NOTES

NOTES

NOTES